SOFTWARE FAILURE: MANAGEMENT FAILURE

Amazing stories and cautionary tales

· · · · · · · · · · · · · · · · ·

Stephen Flowers

University of Brighton, UK

JOHN WILEY & SONS

Chichester · New York · Brisbane · Toronto · Singapore

Other Wiley Editorial Offices

John Wiley & Sons, Inc., 605 Third Avenue,
New York, NY 10158-0012, USA

Jacaranda Wiley Ltd, 33 Park Road, Milton,
Queensland 4064, Australia

John Wiley & Sons (Canada) Ltd, 22 Worcester Road,
Rexdale, Ontario M9W 1L1, Canada

John Wiley & Sons (Asia) Pte Ltd, 2 Clementi Loop #02-01,
Jin Xing Distripark, Singapore 0512

British Library Cataloguing in Publication Data

A catalogue record for this book is available from the British Library

ISBN 0 471 95113 7

Typeset in 12/14pt Bembo by Acorn Bookwork, Salisbury, Wilts
Printed and bound in Great Britain by Bookcraft (Bath) Ltd
This book is printed on acid-free paper responsibly manufactured from sustainable forestation, for which at least two trees are planted for each one used for paper production.

CONTENTS

· · · · · · · · ·

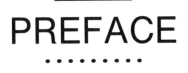

PREFACE

· · · · · · · · ·

This book grew out of a desire to understand why information systems developments sometimes go wrong. What changed this desire into the resolution to produce the book was the realization that there was an almost total absence of detailed case histories of systems development failures. This book is an attempt to fill that gap and share the important management lessons with a wider audience. Indeed, it is my wish that this book will act as an encouragement to the individuals and organizations involved in information systems development to be more open about their failures as well as their successes, so that the whole information systems community may be enriched by their experience.

There is little hard evidence as to exactly how many information systems fail. However, combining the evidence that does exist with anecdotal and off-the-record discussions, it is probably true to say that a significant amount of systems may be labelled as failures for one reason or another. Indeed, the most common response from managers when they learnt that I was writing a book about software development failures was 'Oh, that's very interesting. Are we in it?' Interestingly, nobody suggested that I would have a hard time finding enough material.

In researching this book time and again I came across the strange collusion that exists between the buyers and sellers of information systems. When things go wrong with an information systems development it will almost always result in both sides being eager to bury the facts of the case. Confidentiality agreements, non-disclosure contracts and undisclosed out-of-court settlements are all ways of trying to keep the lid on what is a seething cauldron of failure. And the most likely result of this industrial amnesia? More of the same.

There is also, if we are honest with ourselves, something of the voyeur in all of us. As on a motorway, slowing down to look at an accident, we want to see the wreckage and try to understand what happened before driving on hopefully chastened in the knowledge that, this time, it wasn't us. But while the cases contained within this book may provide a fascinating spectacle to the onlooker, This is not enough. In collecting these cases it is hoped that they will be a modest contribution to the 'folklore' or 'war stories' of the information systems community—the amazing stories and cautionary tales that are a part of every area of human endeavour.

S.F.

February 1996, Brighton

shf@brighton.ac.uk

ACKNOWLEDGEMENTS

· · · · · · · · ·

This book owes a debt to the many people who, at various stages of its inception and creation, offered help, advice and, at times, solace. I would particularly like to thank the following: John Grant of Glaxo Research for his advice, encouragement and comments on drafts of sections of the manuscript; Tony Mann of the University of Greenwich and Rob Kling and the University of Southern California at Irvine for drawing my attention to the Pineapple and MasterNet cases respectively; Nancy Simmons of the GAO for her advice and assistance in the collection of the US Government material and her comments on early parts of the manuscript; Anne Tatalovich of the American Bar Foundation and Marcia Lehr of North West University, among others, for their assistance and advice in the collection of material on the Confirm case; Kevin Turner for his many useful suggestions and late-night discussions out of which came the idea for the development of a set of generic Critical Failure Factors; Marilyn Medforth of the Learning Resources at the University of Brighton for her unstinting help, cooperation and patience; Steve Newman of the University of Brighton Computer Centre for his help in conducting the preliminary research upon which this book is based; my colleagues at the University of Brighton Business School who have been unstinting in their encouragement and advice during the development of this book; the contributors to the RISKS forum and Peter G. Neumann its moderator for providing what was an invaluable resource in the creation of this book—long may you run! I am also grateful to the many consultants and information systems professionals whose advice and experiences helped to shape this book.

This book owes its origins to Rosie Altoft at John Wiley, who also played an important role in turning the original concept into the finished manuscript.

Finally, I thank my partner Claire, without whose support and clear-thinking advice this book would not have been possible.

INTRODUCTION

· · · · · · · · · · · · · · · ·

It's fine to celebrate success but it is more important to heed the lessons of failure.[1]

Good judgement is usually the result of experience. And experience is frequently the result of bad judgement. But to learn from the experience of others requires those who have the experience to share the knowledge with those who follow.[2]

---

[1] (Bill Gates, *The Guardian*, 27 April 1995)
[2] Barry LePatner quoted in To *Engineer is Human: The role of failure in successful design*, Henry Petroski.

Why a Book on Information Systems Failures?

Computerized information systems are at the heart of all modern organizations. Such systems are used as a means of both obtaining competitive advantage and re-engineering the business processes of the organization itself. They have thus become a key component in the success of virtually every business and as the range of computerized applications grows, so too does their importance. Indeed, it is likely that the majority of organizations are becoming increasingly reliant upon their information systems (IS) development efforts to secure their future success.

Yet the total or partial failure of IS developments is endemic throughout the business world. Many millions are wasted every year on systems that either do not perform as expected, do not work at all or are abandoned before they are implemented. When a bridge collapses, a ship sinks, or an airliner falls out of the sky, it is a very public disaster. By comparison, IS disasters are generally private affairs from which individuals and organizations seek to distance themselves in the hope that the details of the failure will soon be forgotten. Therefore while such disasters happen with surprising regularity, very little may be known about the events that contributed to a particular IS failure.

While this closed approach to IS failure may arguably be good for the corporate image, it effectively stunts the development of a widespread management awareness of the pitfalls of IS development. Indeed, it could be argued that one outcome of this approach is that it effectively ensures that business organizations become locked in a cycle of failure, with each condemned to repeat the mistakes of others. Indeed, in the words of George Santayana:

> Progress, far from consisting in change, depends upon retentiveness.
> . . . Those who cannot remember the past are condemned to repeat it.

This book is an attempt to break out of this cycle of failure and forgetfulness by bringing together, often from a diverse range of fragmentary sources, material about a number of significant IS failures. Each IS failure provides the basis for a case study that attempts to give a coherent account of the events surrounding each failure, identifying its major causes, and outlining the management lessons.

There should be no shame (corporate or individual) in failure, for in the words of Edward Phelps: 'The man who makes no mistakes does not usually make anything'. In fact, learning from our failures is an essential part of progress. Success will often tell us what we already know, but failure is just as valuable since it shows us what we have yet to learn. Indeed, according to Bill Gates:

> ...Setbacks are normal, especially among people and companies trying new things.
>
> When employees know that mistakes won't lead to retribution, it creates an atmosphere in which people are willing to come up with ideas and suggest changes. This is important to a company's long-term success. And drawing lessons from mistakes reduces the possibility that errors will be repeated or compounded. (*The Guardian*, 27 April 1995)

Who Should Read This Book?

This book should be read by any manager involved in the procurement of hardware, software, or consultancy to design, develop and install large or small information systems to improve business efficiency. The emphasis is on management skills and tools for analysis and control rather than technical aspects.

Although this book looks at the progress and ultimate failure of a number of information systems projects, the focus is primarily on their managerial rather than technical aspects. Indeed, as you examine each case, you will see that the failures were generally the result of managerial rather than technical problems. The many lessons contained within this book should thus be of great interest to both technical and non-technical managers.

A brief glossary of technical terms is provided as is an annotated bibliography for further reading.

What is an Information Systems Failure?

An information system is some combination of computer hardware, communication technology and software designed to handle information related to one or more business processes. Examples include accounting systems, personnel systems, airline booking systems, automatic teller machine (ATM) systems and sales order processing systems. The software used within such information systems may either be custom-written or purchased off the shelf as 'packaged software'.

The failure of an information system occurs when the system as a whole does not operate as expected and its overall performance is sub-optimal. There are, of course, many degrees of failure, ranging from 'flawed but usable' to 'totally unusable', 'unused', or 'absolute disaster', and while there are probably many flawed information systems in use, it is usually only the absolute disasters that receive wide public attention.

An information system can be termed a failure if, on implementation, it does not perform as originally intended or if it is so user-hostile that it is rejected by users and is under-utilised. An information system may also, technically, be regarded as a failure if the cost of the development exceeds any benefits the system may bring throughout its useful life. A final category of failure is when, due to problems with the complexity of the system or the management of the project, an IS development is abandoned before it is completed. All the case studies examined within this book illustrate at least one of these four categories of failure.

Taking the concept of failure a stage further it is sometimes possible to identify at which stage of the systems development process mistakes were made that contributed to the eventual failure of the system. In analysing IS failures to understand how they occurred, failings in the project initiation, systems analysis/design, programming/testing or implementation stages will be highlighted.

IS failures may thus be viewed at the level of both the final completed system (if it gets that far) and the development stages that it has passed through. To understand the overall scale of the failure it is necessary to look at the system as a whole. To try to gain an understanding of how an IS failure happened, each of the stages in its development must be examined. Each major case study attempts to provide an analysis of the overall scale of the IS failure under examination together with, as far as is possible, a detailed discussion of its causes.

Rationale for Selection of Case Studies

In an attempt to demonstrate that IS failures are widespread throughout business and government a wide-ranging approach has been adopted in the selection and inclusion of case material. The book contains examples of IS failures within the travel, financial, music, healthcare and transport sectors as well as a series of government IS disasters, with the cases being drawn from a number of countries.

While the book contains a large number of examples of IS failures drawn from around the world, the major cases relate to information systems that failed in the UK and the USA in recent years. The five major cases are all examples of large-scale IS failures, including three of major commercial development failures and two relating to government IS failures. This balance between commercial and government IS failures is intentional. Indeed, while government IS failures tend to be more public, commercial failures occur regularly and are generally far more costly, suggesting that lessons need to be learned in both business and government.

The major cases have been selected to demonstrate some of the many facets of IS failure with one, the case of the London Ambulance Service computerized despatch system, being a rare example of a particularly well-documented development. The smaller case studies have been included both to reinforce the points made within the larger cases and as a demonstration that the same mistakes have been made (probably many times) before.

Finally, the book does not contain any examples of defence IS failures. While such disasters have been some of the most costly failures of all time the author has no wish to dilute the many management lessons that may be drawn from the business cases examined. Indeed, while there is probably enough material on defence IS failures alone to write several books on the subject many of the lessons would probably apply only to the Alice in Wonderland world of defence technology.

Structure of the Book

The book is based around five major case-study chapters, with one of these devoted to a discussion of a number of UK and US government IS failures. Each of the major case studies has four main sections in which the details of the case are recounted, the major events surrounding the development listed, the causes of the failure analysed and a series of management lessons drawn. The final chapter of the book attempts to identify a set of core Critical Failure Factors that are intended to be applicable to virtually all IS developments.

An annotated bibliography provides a guide to other publications for those who wish to pursue further the subject of IS failure.

A Note on Sources

The reticence with which virtually the entire commercial sector has on the subject of IS failure in general, and their own IS failures in particular, has meant that in order to produce many of these case studies the author has often had to piece the case together from fragmentary evidence. However, while sufficient material has been available to produce a coherent picture of the progress of the IS development, it is recognized that these accounts are incomplete. A further complication has been the exclusion, on legal advice, of a range of interesting material from the cases. These are the realities of the modern commercial world. However, despite these reservations, the major themes within the developments are apparent and enough detail has been included for a range of useful lessons to be drawn.

Nonetheless, a number of the sources referenced are press reports and it is acknowledged that inaccuracies in the reporting process may exist. If any reader identifies where such errors have crept into the case material in this book the author would be glad to receive details of how they should be changed.

Future Editions

While it is to be hoped that the numbers of IS failures will become fewer over time, it is likely that mistakes will continue to be made. It is thus planned that this book will reappear in an updated form with a range of new examples of IS failures. If you know of a large or small IS failure that you think would form the basis for a case study, or have suggestions for improving the book, the author would like to hear from you. The author can be contacted either c/o the publisher or using e-mail on s.h.flowers@brighton.ac.uk

2

THE PERFORMING RIGHT SOCIETY

PROMS

· · · · · · · · · · · · · · · · ·

Money for nothing?[1]

────── ·······
[1] Taken from the title of a song by Dire Straits, a band whose name is also rather appropriate to the situation in which the PRS found themselves. Incidentally, Dire Straits are a member of the PRS.

Chronology of Major Events

1987–89	Downsizing proposal examined and preliminary designs and investigations take place
May 1990	Detailed Business Case prepared and approved by the PRS Council
	Work begins on PROMS project using specifications prepared in 1989
1990–1991	Quarterly reports to PRS Council confident of success
Sept. 1991	Project Team informs PRS Council of 10-week delay
1991–92	Quarterly reports to PRS Council remain confident of success
Feb. 1992	Original implementation date abandoned
	PRS Council asks for more frequent reports on progress
May 1992	Interim implementation plan submitted to PRS Council
July 1992	More detailed version of implementation plan submitted to PRS Council
Sept. 1992	Independent consultant called in to conduct interim review of project
	Technical assessment of system reveals July plan as inadequate
Oct.–Dec. 92	Senior managers leave PRS
Nov. 1992	New implementation plan created
	Proposed new target date of September 1994 and additional cost of £6 million
	PRS General Council decides to suspend PROMS project indefinitely
	Independent consultant recalled to assess if system can be salvaged
April 1993	Report into PROMS published
	New Chief Executive appointed
Nov. 1993	IT Director appointed
	ICL mainframe purchased
July 1994	PRS reportedly makes £16 million claim for compensation from one of the main PROMS contractors ·

—— The PROMS project is a classic case in which an organization found itself struggling to cope with the demands of an ambitious downsizing project. The case follows the progress of the project and provides an analysis of how the PRS spent over £8 million ($12 million) on a failed development. Important lessons on organisational structure, project reviews and the role of consultants are drawn from the evidence surrounding the case and the changes that resulted within the PRS as a result of the failure are examined in detail. Much of the information in this case comes from *PRS Summary of PROMS Assessment* a summarized version of the report that was decisive in ending the PROMS Project, ... and the *PRS Yearbook 1993–94*.

Introduction

Situated in the heart of London's West End the Performing Right Society (PRS) is an important part of the global entertainment industry. Each time a song is played on the radio or performed at a concert a royalty must be paid to the holder of the copyright and, in the UK, the PRS is the organization that collects those royalties. Established in 1914 as an association of composers, lyricists and publishers, the PRS currently licenses over 16 million compositions covering every type of musical style, from orchestral symphonies to thrash metal, from jazz to advertising jingles. The PRS is affiliated to a large number of similar bodies around the world, including in the USA the American Society of Composers, Authors and Publishers (ASCAP), in Italy the Società Italiana degli Autori ed Editorio (SIAE) and in Australia and New Zealand the Australasian Performing Right Association Ltd (APRA). In 1993 the PRS collected over £155 million ($233 million) both on behalf of their 26 000 UK members and, through their links to affiliate organisations, a further 750 000 copyright holders around the world.

The PRS licenses the playing of recorded music in over 250 000 shops and other premises and will also license more than 40 000 live performances in a typical year. The PRS thus fulfils a complex administrative role, acting as the primary collector and distributor of royalties and the guardian of musical performance rights.

The Performing Right Society is a non-profit-making organization controlled by a General Council of non-executive directors guided by a Chair and two Deputy Chairs. The General Council is responsible for administration and the formulation of policy, and its composition is split evenly between music writers and publishers, all of whom are elected from among the membership. The management responsible for the day-to-day running of the PRS is appointed by the Council, with the Chief Executive leading a team of executive directors in charge of the major divisions within the organization. At the time of commencing the PROMS development the PRS did not have an IT Director.

The PROMS Development

The PRS has long made use of computer systems to enable it to perform its complex administrative responsibilities and by the latter part of the 1980s had several applications running on separate mainframe computers. The Performing Right On-line Membership System, or PROMS, was conceived in 1987 as part of a strategy that would see the PRS end its reliance upon mainframe computers and replace its major applications with a single large database. The rationale for making such a move was that it would enable the organization to base its administrative systems on powerful minicomputers running UNIX, thereby enabling the PRS to move their operations away from the proprietary mainframe environment and into the world of 'open' systems. In the jargon of the time, the PRS was attempting to 'downsize' its operations.

The idea behind downsizing, when used in relation to computer systems, is that the increasing power of hardware makes it technically feasible to run mainframe applications on minicomputers, or minicomputer-based systems, onto networks of PCs without any loss of performance. The payoffs from making such a move are the large savings in software, hardware and staffing costs that are said to result.

Downsizing from a mainframe to a minicomputer may also involve moving from (expensive) proprietary mainframe-based systems to software that operates within the 'open' UNIX environment. The benefits of such a move are, in theory, that the move to a UNIX environment enables organizations to reduce costs by use of the less expensive software available.

At the time of the original proposals the PRS depended upon separate

ICL mainframe computers to run their large file-based licensing and membership applications. The development of PROMS would not only enable the PRS to discard these mainframes but would also combine the data held in these separate systems into the PROMS database. It was intended that the development of PROMS and the move to minicomputer systems would reduce the problems associated with maintaining multiple sets of identical information held on separate records over several existing computer systems. The PROMS proposal would also lead to a reduction in operational costs due to lower expenses associated with hardware and software as well as lower administration and staff costs. In all, it was estimated by the PRS that the adoption of the PROMS proposal would cut its £25 million ($38 million) administration costs by up to £4 million ($6 million) a year.

Once it was fully operational the demands to be placed on the new PROMS system were to be considerable. The system was to be designed to be able to handle the workload generated by up to 300 users (100 active users and up to 200 *ad-hoc* users), all of whom would be working at the same time on the central 40Gb PROMS relational database. In order to ensure adequate response times to such a large number of concurrent users such a system, termed an On-line Transaction Processing (OLTP) application, requires a very powerful combination of hardware/software. At the time PROMS was being proposed there was much debate within the computer industry as to the feasibility of downsizing such demanding OLTP applications onto minicomputers running under UNIX, and successful examples were few and far between. It was therefore recognized at the time of its initial proposal that PROMS would be an ambitious system.

In order to be successful PROMS would require an optimal combination of hardware and software that would result only from careful design and planning. Between 1987 and 1989 the in-house systems staff at PRS undertook, with assistance from external consultants, a series of investigations and preliminary designs as they tried to establish the feasibility of the proposed downsizing move. During this initial phase a series of detailed preparatory specifications for both the software designs and the hardware on which it was to run were prepared.

This initial preparatory work was subsequently to form the basis of a detailed report that was shown in early 1990 to senior managers within the PRS. Given the complex and highly technical nature of the report, a detailed review of the proposals was undertaken by external consultants. It was only after this process had been successfully completed that the final version of the report was summarized to form the basis of a Business Case. In May 1990, having considered the Business Case in some detail, the PRS General Council gave its approval and PROMS was born. The implementation date for the new system was to be March 1992.

Although it is not known how precise the original Business Case was on the projected overall cost of the project, it was subsequently revealed (Collins, 1993) that the system was to be delivered on a time-and-materials basis, with contractors being paid according to the amount of work done, rather than by what they delivered. In order that the progress of the project could be monitored, the senior manager heading development was instructed to make quarterly progress reports to the General Council.

Once PROMS was given the go-ahead by the General Council, hardware was purchased and contractors were engaged to work on various components of the overall system. Much of the activity that took place in the early months of the project was based directly upon the preparatory work that had been undertaken before the project was approved. Custom software was written according to the specifications that had been prepared in the year before the project was approved. Computer hardware and proprietary software were also purchased largely in the way selected in 1989.

During 1990 and 1991 the quarterly reports to the General Council remained confident on the progress being made with PROMS.

Work appeared to proceed smoothly on the PROMS system until the autumn of 1991, when at the quarterly review meeting the General Council was informed of a ten-week delay due to software difficulties. However, behind the scenes a number of serious problems had begun to have an impact on the project.

It was reported that a fundamental problem with the system was in the design of important parts of the database. The contractor responsible for designing the database had apparently been provided with insufficient information with which to work and had thus made a series of assumptions in order to complete the task. Some of these assumptions turned out to be incorrect, with the result that the database design was inefficient with response times of up to 30 minutes (Collins, 1994, p. 1).

A second problem related to the choice of hardware upon which the completed system was supposed to run. Central to the downsizing strategy was the acquisition of hardware powerful enough to run the large PROMS relational database with adequate response times. It had emerged that 'benchmarking' tests[2] had revealed that even the largest UNIX systems available from Pyramid and Hewlett-Packard would not be powerful enough to run PROMS (Collins, 1992, p. 1).

The final problem related to the quality of the data held within the existing membership and licensing systems. It had been impossible to move the data across from the existing applications to the PROMS system due to the fact that it was both incomplete and also apparently contained large numbers of errors and inconsistencies. Even if the data to be moved across had been of sufficient quality, to do so it still would have been impossible since the system itself was unfinished.

Work continued on the system until February 1992 when, with just six weeks to go, the project team were forced to abandon the March implementation date. Managers working on the project had then to struggle to produce a new project plan, with interim and detailed plans being submitted to the General Council in May and July respectively. By this time the concern felt within the Council was such that it was calling for monthly progress reports, and it was beginning to question different aspects of the project.

Over the summer of 1992 further problems arose with the hardware, software and the data files and in September an independent consultant was called in to conduct an interim review of the project. The ensuing assessment of the system revealed the July plan to be inadequate. The suspension of the project was resisted at this stage and a final plan produced by the managers running PROMS in November proposed that a further £6 million ($9 million) to be spent in order to complete the system by the new implementation date of September 1994. However, by this time it was all too late, and the General Council made

---

[2] When selecting the hardware appropriate for a large application it is usual to make use of software tools to simulate the loading under which that hardware will have to operate. The use of such capacity planning software enables potential buyers to test the performance of hardware in a variety of situations to evaluate its suitability.

the brave decision to suspend the project. Shortly after this decision was taken the independent consultant was recalled to assess whether the system could be salvaged.

By the time the PROMS project was suspended in September 1992 some £11 million ($17 million) had been spent since work had commenced over two and a half years earlier.

In the wake of the PROMS disaster many senior PRS managers who had been involved with the project left the organization, a computer-literate Chief Executive was appointed, and a large-scale review of management functions undertaken. The subsequent appointment of an IT Director was a direct reaction to the PROMS disaster. One of the first acts of the new IT Director was to place an order for a new ICL mainframe.

In July 1994 the PRS opened discussions with the contractor responsible for project management, one of the 26 consultancy firms involved in the failed project. Although the level of compensation sought by the PRS was not made public, it was reported that the PRS had made a claim of £7.9 million ($11.9 million) for recovery of sums spent on the project plus a further £8 million ($12 million) of consequential costs (Collins, 1994, p. 1). The discussions between the firms ended inconclusively in December of that year.

Causes of the PROMS Failure[3]

As a result of the problems that had occurred with PROMS, and the large amount of money that had been spent, the General Council commissioned an external consultant to provide a technical evaluation of the project. What makes the PROMS project unusual, given that it occurred within a commercial organization, is the fact that a summary of the findings of the external consultant instrumental in ending the development was made public.[4] Such openness is exceptional within commercial organizations and is perhaps explained by the democratic nature of the PRS.

————————·······

[3]The quotes in this section come from *PRS Summary of PROMS Assessment*.
[4]An edited version of the full report *PRS Summary of PROMS Assessment* was sent to all members of the PRS.

A Question of Competence?

The PROMS project is an example of a large systems development project going badly wrong. The PRS Summary Report makes claims that there were inadequacies in the behaviour of the managers responsible for the project:

> ...None of the most senior managers who were involved with PROMS displayed an understanding of the needs of large development projects or the needs of information technology. They acted as if nothing serious was wrong...

> The project was fundamentally flawed when the managers commended it to the Council in 1990, and thereafter they presided over an expensive failure.

The PRS Summary Report lists five major failings in the work of the management in charge of the project. They failed:

- To set out the requirements in a form that could be understood and checked by ordinary people
- To survey in sufficient detail the information that would be processed
- To produce a coherent design for the whole system
- To control the work of the project team
- To inform the Council of the state of the project.

In defence of the managers involved, such comments are easily made with hindsight. Why these things were not spotted at the time is, in this context, the big question.

Advice

It could not be said that the PRS rushed into the PROMS project. The original proposal was prepared over a long period with the help of external experts. Following such preparation the General Council's approval of the project must have seemed a safe and well-founded decision, with the request for quarterly progress reports a wise precaution.

It is likely that the General Council was initially reasonably confident that it had made the correct decision. However, the PRS Summary Report suggests that the PRS did not receive the best advice in three important areas: project feasibility, project management, and in the design of the PROMS database.

Project Feasibility

In the early stages of the project, after the preliminary work of 1987–9 had been completed, a detailed report based on this work was presented to senior managers. This report was subsequently to be reviewed by external consultants before a formal Business Case was presented to the General Council. This was done by the same consultants used for the preparatory work.

Project Management

A project as large and complex as PROMS is heavily reliant upon project planning and project management to stand any realistic chance of success. An important part of planning and managing a software development project is the identification at an early stage of problems that, uncorrected, may affect the critical path of the plan and ultimately the date of implementation. It appears that the serious problems that existed within the PROMS development were not identified.

The implications of failing to identify problems within a project is that, when they are finally discovered, it is highly likely that a lot of the system will have to be reworked, with obvious repercussions for the project plan.

Database Design

Given the scale and complexity of the problems the PROMS system was attempting to solve, the design of the database would inevitably be a factor critical to the success of the project. However, a crucial flaw in the project was that the information required to design the database was inadequate:

> A contractor was retained to design the physical details of the database. The contractor was given insufficient information to do this properly. As a result assumptions were made which in some cases have since been shown to be wrong. The database design is inefficient. In circumstances such as those of 1990 PRS managers should have been warned of the risks of proceeding to design the database and build the application software with insufficient information. No record of such a warning has been found.

One might conclude that this extract from the PRS Summary Report illustrates severe weaknesses both in the design process and in the communications between PRS managers and contractors.

Attitude Problems

Perhaps most damning of all the criticisms contained in the PRS Summary Report are the comments on the attitude that existed among staff at all levels within the PRS itself.

> The prevailing attitude of staff and managers in the PRS has been found not to be conducive to the successful conduct of large-scale computer projects. That requires the managers and staff concerned to be open about mistakes and failures, to learn from them, to be willing to expose their work to review by their peers, to welcome criticism, and to have the capacity to accept responsibility themselves for the work they and their staff do. If, as seems likely, this was also true in 1990 then the prevailing attitude would have contributed to the failure of the PROMS project.

This is perhaps the key issue in enabling us to understand how the PROMS development became an expensive failure. Staff attitude is simply a reflection of the much larger issue of organizational culture, with the latter largely determining the former. If the attitude of staff was indeed not conducive to the successful conduct of large-scale computer projects, then it is very unlikely that it would be conducive to the successful conduct of any significant project. If this is true, it is highly probable that problems surrounding the organizational focus, professionalism and accountability existed within the PRS prior to the PROMS project. It is therefore also likely that it was only as a result of the failure of PROMS that these negative aspects of the culture within the PRS became apparent and that steps could be taken to effect change.

As has been discussed earlier, the General Council, elected by the PRS membership, is responsible for both administration and the formulation of policy. However, the PRS was run on a day-to-day basis by the Chief Executive together with a number of executive directors. Throughout the PROMS development there appears to have been a tension between these two groups.

The impression one gains is that of an executive management in a position to prevent the General Council from gaining access to the organization they are supposed to control. It appears that the balance of power between the executive managers and General Council was weighted in favour of the executive and that the Council was unable to gain control without a hard fight. If this analysis is correct, then it becomes easier to understand how a project that was apparently flawed from the beginning could continue for nearly two years before it was suspended.

Lessons of the PROMS Experience

The PROMS debacle clearly represented a crisis point in the life of PRS as an organization and became a catalyst enabling a series of changes to take place. The organization has obviously learnt a number of painful lessons, but it has also demonstrated a positive willingness to learn from the mistakes that were made. The Chairman of the PRS was to write of the PROMS failure: 'I trust we have learnt a vitally important lesson, and that we will use what we have learned to ensure that a mistake such as this will never happen again' (Bickerton, 1993/4).

The following sections will not only discuss the lessons that may be learnt from the PROMS experience but will also examine some of the organizational and personnel changes that were subsequently made by the PRS as a direct reaction to the failure.

Organizational Lessons

Organizational Culture

It is suggested that the culture prevailing within the PRS up to the PROMS failure had led to tensions between the General Council and senior management. One source of the tensions could have been the requirement for the 'professional' managers running the PRS to account for their actions to a General Council remote from their work. Such a situation could easily result in the PRS management developing, over time, the self-serving attitude common to many bureaucracies.

Once such a culture develops, a rift will inevitably open up between those that manage an organization on a day-to-day basis and those for whose benefit the organization is supposed to be run. One way of avoiding the worst effects of such a situation is to refocus the basic aims of the organization towards beneficial goals.

The PRS has attempted to achieve this transformation by undertaking a fundamental examination of what they do, how it is done, and for what purpose, at every level of the organization. The aim of this wide-ranging re-examination is the development of a culture based on 'total continuous improvement' for the benefit of members. A major part of this strategy is the development of defined and measurable levels of performance for the services provided to the PRS membership. In broad terms it could be said that the PRS was attempting to become a customer-focused organization.

Organizational Structure

The relationship between the senior executive managers and the General Council of the PRS may have been a factor that contributed to the PROMS project lasting as long as it did. In the period following the PROMS failure the management structure was reorganized and a closer relationship formed between PRS senior management and the General Council.

An IS Steering Group was also set up whose terms of reference include the requirement to integrate the results of a revised PRS Information System and Technology strategy with the recommendations made by the external consultant who examined the PROMS development. This was composed of senior and middle managers with a wide range of experience in finance, project development, membership services, repertoire and performances.

Finally, as part of its thorough re-examination of the what, how and why of the work that the PRS actually does, a Business Processes Review was established. The purpose of this review was to investigate business processes throughout the organization in order to identify where and how it will be possible to improve the levels of service offered to the PRS membership. It is the intention that this parallel review should provide a basis for the work of the IS Steering Group, some of whose members it shares.

Staffing

A problem faced by many organizations, and one that may be most acute at the highest levels of management, is a lack of any real understanding of the role of IT and the requirements of IT projects. It is possible that IT specialists will, consciously or unconsciously, foster this state of affairs in order to ensure that they secure and retain a high degree of autonomy. While this has many short-term attractions for managers, enabling them to delegate knotty IT-related problems to specialists who will somehow solve them, it also has a number of short- and long-term dangers.

The major short-term danger is that IT staff will waste large amounts of money pursuing a mirage to little effect. A secondary danger is that the specialists in whom a great deal has been invested will leave the organization, taking their expertise with them. The longer-term problems are perhaps more severe. By leaving IT to the specialist it is likely that the explicit (or implicit) IT strategy adopted may become technology-led rather than business-led. This is likely to result in a range of information systems that each have a high degree of technical merit or interest but are not business-facing. A secondary long-term problem is that the organization, and the staff at all levels within it, are denied opportunities for development. A likely outcome from this state of affairs is the creation of a technology-averse culture within an organization. This will not only reinforce the IT-specialist–business divisions but it is also likely to result in a failure to identify the innovative IT opportunities that often come from the non-specialists within an organization.

This danger is recognized within the PRS Summary Report in that it recommends that the PRS undertake a comprehensive training programme to change the attitudes of ... managers and staff, and equip them to make good use of information technology in the future. In addition, since the PROMS failure, the PRS has made a large number of senior management changes, appointing a new Chief Executive with experience of change management and the implementation of computer systems. And, in a move that brought IT to the centre of senior management activities, in November 1993 the PRS appointed an IT Director.

Project Reviews

It is an obvious fact that is well worth restating—corrective action taken at an early stage in the life of an IS development is far cheaper than if it is taken very late. As result of the PRS Summary Report it is possible to put some figures alongside what is a well-understood, but often ignored, aphorism.

Of the £11 million ($16.5 million) spent over the duration of the PROMS project, £8 million ($12 million) was wasted. It was estimated that, had an independent review taken place in December 1990 it would have cost less than £200 000 ($300 000), but would probably have revealed the faults that were to emerge nearly two years later. In this case an early review would have cost 2.5% of the amount of money that was eventually wasted on the PROMS project. However you look at this figure, an early project review has to be a good investment.

Human Factors

The *Titanic* Effect[5]

> I cannot imagine any condition which could cause this ship to flounder. I cannot conceive of any vital disaster happening to this vessel. (E. J. Smith, Captain of the *Titanic*, 1912)

It is an observable fact that those who are most closely concerned with a

---

[5] The *Titanic* Effect: The severity with which a system fails is directly proportional to the intensity of the designer's belief that it cannot. Original source unknown, but it is quoted in ACM SIGSOFT (1986, p. 14).

project/enterprise/development/relationship are often the last people to see its inherent problems. There is something about the amount of emotional investment that we put into the activities with which we are involved that makes it impossible to make an impartial assessment of their strengths and weaknesses. But it is unfortunately also often true that the worse things look with our project/enterprise/development/relationship, the more we cling to the small chance that it will, after all, turn out well, rather than address the mounting weight of evidence that it almost certainly will not.

In the face of such potential for such commitment to a course of action it is vital that the work of project teams takes place in an atmosphere of openness, ensuring that reality acts as a benchmark for the decision-making process.

The Lure of the Leading Edge

It is probable that part of the attraction for the managers involved in any ground-breaking project was the opportunity to work at the leading edge of technology. By the late 1980s there were very few examples of large-scale OLTP systems having been downsized onto minicomputers running the UNIX operating system. The opportunity to be involved in such a project would have been attractive both to the managers involved and to the specialist consultants that they employed to advise them. An obvious danger with such a project was that the downsizing solution could have acquired such a momentum that all other potential solutions would have been ignored.

Certainly, while the PRS realized that PROMS was an ambitious project, it is debatable if it was fully understood by all involved just how close (or even beyond) the leading edge the proposal actually was:

> Little did the society realize the extent to which it would be *pioneering* large on-line transaction processing systems running under UNIX [my emphasis].[6]

The danger, as illustrated in the above quote, is when a leading-edge project turns out to be a pioneering approach to a problem about

————————........

[6] Roger Burford, then Technical Director of Data Logic, quoted in Collins, T. 'Royalties group in dire straits over UNIX plans', Computer Weekly, 17 Septembser 1992, p1.

which, inevitably, few of the answers, let alone all the problems, are fully understood.

Consultants

Consultants are widely used within IS developments. They often offer a range of skills and experience that organizations are unlikely to have in-house, and provide an opportunity to gain access to the latest IS tools and techniques. Consultants can, at a price, provide everything from a complete design, build and implementation service to expertise in specific areas of a project. Given the fast-moving nature of the IT industry, consultancies are often a preferred option. However, as we have seen, consultancies cannot guarantee success.

The PROMS report suggested that the principal advisor chosen by management to examine the feasibility of the proposals had also been involved in their preparation. If this is indeed the case then impartiality would have been difficult, and many would consider it to be be unprofessional conduct to accept such a dual commission, however well intentioned. Impartial advice at an early stage of any project proposal can help non-specialist management to put the project in context and can signal the need for close inspection and review of specific aspects or indeed for further research before the project begins.

VARIATIONS ON A THEME

The problems with the failed PROMS downsizing project may well echo in your mind as you read the following report of another downsizing project that ended in failure.

The California DMV Disaster[7]

> We tried to throw the long ball from the backfield up to the front, and that kind of strategy is fraught with peril.[8]

---

[7] Much of the detail in this case comes from Bozman (1994a,b)
[8] Evan Nossoff, DMV spokesman, quoted in Bozman (1994a).

The California Department of Motor Vehicles (DMV) is responsible for handling the State of California's 50 million vehicle registrations and driver's licences and the annual collection of over $5 billion in taxes and fees. By the late 1980s the system that supported this operation, parts of it dating back to the 1960s, was showing its age and the decision to upgrade it was taken. The aging system, a hotch-potch of flat-file databases and applications written in assembler language running on obsolete mainframes, was to be redeveloped around the use of the latest relational database systems and powerful minicomputer technology.

Commencing in 1989, the external consultants (Ernst & Young) called in to manage the project withdrew in 1990, with DMV itself taking over the management of the project. DMV staff also managed the development of the application programs that would be developed using a CASE (Computer Aided Software Engineering) tool, Texas Instruments Inc.'s Information Engineering Facility. Unfortunately, it appears that DMV staff had little experience of using IEF and faced a difficult task, and in May 1994, after $44 million ($29.3 million) had been spent and not a single application program written, the state government halted the project.

The reasons behind the development failure will be uncovered by independent consultants called in to review the project—at a cost of $500 000 (£330 000). According to the DMV's manager of Information Systems the project had three strikes against it:

> Strike one was how we started out, without full enough reasons for what we wanted to do. Strike two was Ernst & Young's withdrawing from the project, and we didn't fully understand what that would mean. ... Strike three was our inability to get an operational system.

One immediate result of the failure was the California Legislature's wish to review the state's $1.2 billion information technology budget.

References

ACM SIGSOFT, *Software Engineering Notes*, **11**, No. 1, January, 14 (1986).
Bickerton, W., 'The Chairman's Foreword', *PRS Yearbook '93–'94*, 5.
Bozman, J., 'DMV disaster—California kills failed $44m project', *Computerworld*, 9 May (1994a).

Bozman, J., 'California projects mismanaged—lawmakers accuse Technology Office of missspending funds', *Computerworld*, 23 May (1994b).

Collins, T., 'Royalties group in dire straits over UNIX plans', *Computer Weekly*, 17 September (1992).

Collins, T., 'PRS salvages 20% of downsized software', *Computer Weekly*, 11 March (1993).

Collins, T., 'PRS makes record £16m claim for compensation', *Computer Weekly*, 14 July (1994).

CONFIRM
Computerized reservation system

· · · · · · · · · · · · · · · · · ·

A broken Sabre?

Chronology of Major Events

March 1988	AMR, Marriott Corp., Budget Rent a Car Corp., and Hilton Hotels announce joint venture to produce a computer reservations system for rental cars and hotel rooms
May 1990	Project said to be on track for going live in early 1992. Development now undertaken by a joint venture company called Intrico
April 1992	Confirm commences beta testing at Hilton Hotels Corp. Problems with the system begin to emerge
May 1992	Software compatibility problems are discovered within Confirm, 18-month delay announced
	After a review big staff changes take place, with over 20 reassigned and 8 leaving the organization
June 1992	Budget Rent a Car and Hilton Hotels withdraw from the project
	AMR and Marriott to continue with Confirm
	Development work on Confirm is suspended
July 1992	AA announces a $166 million (£115 million) loss for the second quarter of 1992. Of this amount $109 million (£70 million) was a one-off charge against anticipated losses from the Confirm system
Sept. 1992– April 1993	Flurry of litigation between the partners as damages are sought due to the collapse of Confirm
Nov. 1992	Litigation goes to mediation
Jan. 1993	AMR announce a $935 million (£617 million) loss for 1992, of which $213 million (£142 million) related to a write-off on the Confirm system
Jan. 1994	An out-of-court settlement is agreed between all parties

—— This case charts the history of what was reportedly one of the most costly commercial systems development failures of all time. The Confirm project started out as an ambitious joint venture but ended up in a flurry of writs as the partners sued and countersued over the disaster. The case examines the progress of the project and provides an analysis of how the development failed. The major lessons of the experience, relating to the establishment of joint ventures, weaknesses in organisational culture and other problems are discussed. (The Confirm system was such big news in the US business community that its development, and subsequent demise, was reported by newspapers as diverse as the *Wall Street* Journal, the *Washington Times*, the San José Mercury ...... *News* and *USA Today*.

Introduction

American Airlines' SABRE computer reservation system has achieved a legendary status in the computer industry. Any discussion of how technology can provide competitive advantage will almost certainly make reference to the way in which SABRE dominated the airline business to such an extent that it became more profitable than the airline that created it. The impact of SABRE on air travel in the USA was huge and it was a key factor in enabling American Airlines (AA) to overtake United Airlines and achieve the largest share of the US market. The importance of SABRE was such that Robert Crandall, then American's CEO (Chief Executive Officer), is said to have once remarked that if forced to choose between the reservation system and the transport business, he would keep SABRE and sell the airline.

The competitive edge that SABRE gave AA was not just from providing a convenient method of booking airline seats, but came from intelligent use of the information the system contained. A central element of SABRE is the yield management system that provides the ability to maximize the revenue obtained from every seat on every flight offered. In addition to calculating optimal seat revenue, the yield management system also examines the fares offered by competitors to ensure that the prices set are competitive.

As SABRE was developed over the years the range of customer services it was able to offer increased dramatically. In addition to the huge array of flight information handled it also offered the ability to book everything from hotel rooms to theatre tickets, and obtain information on everything from European cities to the weather. However, towards the end of the 1980's AA decided that the scope for the future development of SABRE was limited and that the competitive edge it provided was not sustainable over the long term. At around this time AMRIS (AMR Information Systems—the information systems division of AA's parent company that had developed the SABRE system) began to diversify its activities in a series of ventures that exploited its strength in computer services. Activities included creating SABRE-like CRS for the new French high-speed railway (see Socrates case study) and a number of other airlines, as well as embarking on a joint venture with CSX Corp. to market the Encompass freight-tracking system. AMRIS also began to sell network services and offer its data-entry capability to other organizations. The Confirm joint venture was thus part of a wider expansionist strategy for AMRIS and the parent company AMR.

A Short History of SABRE[1]

SABRE, an acronym for Semi-Automated Business Research Environment, was the first computerized reservation system (CRS) to be widely available within the travel industry. First becoming operational for AA in 1962 it was not until the mid-1970s that, after attempts to develop an industry-wide CRS had failed, AA won the race to get its system into the market first. Within a year AA had installed SABRE into more than 130 travel agents' offices free of charge, leaving Delta Airlines and its Apollo system a long way behind. This initial advantage was continued in successive years enabling AA to use SABRE as a means to increase its market share.

Initially, AA had estimated that SABRE would generate $3.1 million (£2 million) in additional sales. This proved to be a wild underestimate since even before the installation programme was complete this was increased to $20.1 million (£13.5 million). A major contributory factor in the rapid rise in business was that, although SABRE showed all

————————........

[1] The information in this section is from SABRE background briefing notes produced by AA and Copeland and McKenney (1988).

flights, AA's were always on the first screen. This was a big advantage since 70% of all bookings were for flights shown on the first screen. Ultimately, some years later, AA overtook Delta Airlines and achieved the largest market share in the USA, with SABRE playing a key role in this achievement.

By 1979 over 1000 travel agents had installed SABRE, by the early 1990s this figure had increased to more than 20 000 agents in over 50 countries around the world.

The Confirm Development

The announcement in March 1988 that some of the largest hotel and travel companies in the USA were to create a computer reservation system for hotel rooms and rental cars was an event full of significance for the industry as a whole. Hilton Hotels Corp., Marriott Corp., Budget Rent a Car and, most importantly, AMR Information Services (like AA, a subsidiary of AMR Corporation) had entered into a partnership to develop a SABRE-like system called Confirm whose services would be available to all hotel and car rental firms. The creation of the Confirm CRS was a clear attempt to do for Hilton, Marriott and Budget what SABRE had done for AA—obtain a significant competitive advantage that could be translated into market dominance.

The opportunity to create Confirm existed because systems like SABRE, although offering a limited hotel and car rental service, could not hope to maintain complete information on types, rates or availability. The proposed hotel/car-rental CRS Confirm would be a full-function system designed to handle the full complexity of hotel and car rental rates together with detailed information on the services offered. For the customer Confirm would provide on-line information about room or car availability, details of special offers available, together with an efficient means of making room or car bookings. For the hotel or car-rental company Confirm would offer a means of defending market share, building detailed profiles of consumer preferences, and the opportunity of achieving gains in efficiency through the use of Confirm's yield management system. It was planned that Confirm, in common with CRSs like SABRE, would be based around a centralized IBM mainframe system that would hold the enormous volume of information provided by hotels and car rental companies. Confirm would be accessible to both travel agencies and corporate travel departments in addition to a large number of other potential users via terminals linked to existing reservation systems.

Writing in the *Harvard Business Review*, Max D. Hopper, then senior vice president for information systems at American Airlines, a subsidiary of AMR Corporation, and vice chairman of AMR Information Services, said of Confirm:

> Its power and sophistication will exceed anything currently available. We expect that the introduction of the Confirm system, scheduled for 1991, will affect pricing strategies and marketing techniques in the hotel and rental car industries in much the same way Apollo and SABRE transformed the airline business (Hopper, 1990).

The stage was thus set for the creation of Confirm, the system that was intended to play an important role in the hotel and car-rental business.

The Confirm project was conceived as a joint development between AMRIS, Budget Rent a Car, Hilton Hotels and Marriott, with the work being undertaken by a separate entity called the ABHM Partnership, later renamed the International Reservations and Information Consortium (Intrico). AMRIS was to play two roles in the project, acting as a partner in the joint venture as well as the primary developer of the Confirm system. The Intrico Board (on which AMRIS was represented) was to have overall control of the development.

The project was based at the Intrico site in Carrollton, Texas, with development work being undertaken using an IBM 3090 mainframe computer and Texas Instrument's IEF (Information Engineering Facility) CASE tool. For the Confirm project the decision was made to implement a version of IEF in which it generated its own database structures.

The scale of the development was considerable with up to 500 staff from the four partners working on the project, including around 200 programmers, most of whom came from AMRIS. The other partners in the project provided feedback about the development of the Confirm system through IBM's widely used Joint Application Design Methodology.

Confirm was designed to run on two linked IBM 3090 mainframes. One of these two computers, running IBM's Transaction Processing Facility operating system, would handle the central reservation system (to be written in the C programming language) and maintain records of room and car status and availability. The second mainframe, running under the MVS operating system, was to handle the many DB2 relational databases that would hold information on pricing, customer histories and marketing analysis. A key component of the overall design was the Transaction Management Function (TMF). The TMF, a suite of programs to be developed using the IEF CASE tool, would be the main link between the two systems and the outside world. The TMF program would handle the interface with five major airline reservations systems, provide links to the large number of hotel management systems and all user terminals, and coordinate all communications traffic. The TMF was essential for the operation of the Confirm system. The overall structure of the Confirm system is illustrated in Figure 3.1. The budget for the Confirm development was $125 million (£83 million).

From its start in 1988 work on the Confirm system progressed with few external signs of activity. However, in May 1990 the group convened a press conference to announce that the project had entered

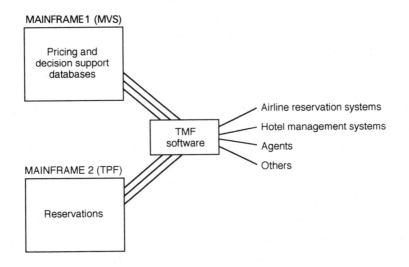

Figure 3.1 Structure of the Confirm system

the programming stage and was on course for the 1992 delivery date. Russell J. Harrison, president of AMRIS is quoted as saying We realize that it's been two years since we've said anything publicly, so we wanted to let everyone know that we're going ahead, we're on time, and we four partners still like each other and are working well together (quoted in *Computerworld*, 1990).

There was some speculation in press reports both at the time and subsequently (*Business Week*, 1994) that an early project review undertaken by IBM in 1989 had suggested the need for corrective action on issues such as quality control, staff awareness and project management. It would be surprising if, in a project of this size and complexity, reviews did not make recommendations for improvement. Given the lack of access to the actual review reports it is impossible to judge whether or not the project was showing early signs of trouble.

At the start of 1992 enough of the Confirm system was available to commence beta-testing[2] by Hilton Hotels Corp. in June. However, the findings of a team of technical experts from SABRE who carried out an audit of Confirm indicated that there were major problems with the system.

When the time came to plug the two main parts (the reservation system and the pricing system) together, they would not work with each other. The two sub-systems, running on different mainframes, relied upon the TMF to act as a bridge between them, handling all communications. It became clear, however, that although some communication was possible with very slow response times, other parts of the system could not access information using the TMF bridge at all.

The major problems with Confirm were associated with the operation of the TMF sub-system. One problem related to the underestimation of the complexity of providing an application-to-application link between the mainframe processors for 60 applications. Another problem was the decision by Intrico to use a CASE tool to automate generation of program code when writing the TMF sub-system. Fundamentally, the TMF did not work as expected.

———————........

[2] Once software has been tested by its creators, termed 'alpha-testing', and the bugs eliminated it may be then passed to a group of users to be tested in a 'live' situation. This is termed 'beta-testing'.

A final problem related to the ability of the Confirm DB2 database to restart and continue operation in the event of a system crash. The problem related to the decision to let the IEF CASE tool generate its own database structure, rather than to implement a structure dictated by the design team. The resulting database was apparently virtually irrecoverable after a crash.

Once the scale of the problems was recognized a staffing review was undertaken in which over 20 IS managers were reassigned, and a further eight left the organisation. The reasons for these staff changes are not known.

As a result of the major problems that had been identified with Confirm it was estimated that 18 months additional work would be required before the system was ready. This delay would push the implementation date to the end of 1993.

By the middle of 1992, after problems with Confirm had been made public, the Intrico partnership had all but collapsed with Hilton, Budget and Marriott all announcing that they were dropping out of the project. AMRIS, the sole remaining partner in the project, continued for a few weeks to work on alone before it announced that it too was to end its development effort on Confirm.

The year 1992 was a bad one for AMR with the company making a $935 million (£622 million) net loss, following on from a loss of $240 million (£160 million) in 1991. A significant part of the $935 million (£622 million) was a write off of $213 million (£142 million) that related to the failure of the Confirm project.

After several months of negotiation between the partners over the failed project the legal wrangles began. Beginning in the fall/autumn of 1992 the following lawsuits were filed:

> AMRIS sued Hilton, Marriot and Budget for $70 million (£48 million)
> Hilton countersued AMRIS for $175 million (£116 million)
> Marriott countersued AMRIS for $65 million (£42 million)
> Budget countersued AMRIS for over $500 million (£335 million)

After the failure of repeated attempts at mediation a date was set for a jury trial (10 January 1994). However, the participants finally settled their differences out of court.

The lawsuits filed are so voluminous they take up many feet of shelf space in various state District courts where they are freely available to anyone with the time and the inclination to pore over them. As is usual in cases like this, the implication of the parties settling their differences out of court means that there is no publicly available independent assessment of the claims made; and no unequivocal analysis is possible of the reasons for failure. As in so many cases, there is only incomplete evidence on which to base advice to avoid similar mishaps.

For those interested in a more detailed coverage of events than is possible here I would recommend the following sources:

> 'Sanctions motion hinges on lost e-mail', *New Jersey Law Journal*, 13 December 1993 (includes a particularly interesting discussion on the role of e-mail messages as potential evidence in such cases)
> 'Software nightmare comes alive for airline', *San José Mercury News*, 20 July 1992, p.9.
> 'Portrait of a project as a total disaster', *Business Week*, 17 January 1994, p.36.
> 'AMR sues partners. Mainframes won't co-ordinate', *Technical Computing*, 1 November 1992
> 'The collapse of Confirm', *Information Week*, 12 October 1992, p.12
> 'When professional standards are lax: The CONFIRM failure and its lessons' *Communications of the AGM*, October 1994, p. 29

From the many newspaper reports at the time it would seem the points of dispute included:

- Definition of system functionality
- Missed deadlines
- Requests for specificiation changes
- Overwhelming numbers of change requests
- The reporting procedures for technical and scheduling problems
- Project management skills
- Suitability of managers from all participants involved (for various reasons including knowledge of existing systems as well as development)
- Choice and use of development tools
- Poor communication between the various partners.

Causes of the Confirm Disaster[3]

Given the huge reputation that AMR and SABRE enjoyed within the IS industry until the Confirm debacle, it is initially hard to imagine how such an unmitigated disaster could occur. Indeed, AMR and AA had benefited from a 'halo effect' arising from its amazingly successful SABRE system. Writing in the *Harvard Business Review*, Max Hopper, then senior vice president for information systems at AA and vice chairman of AMR Information Services, said:

> At American Airlines...we have spent 30 years handcrafting computer systems. We like to think we're better at this than most and that our skills in hardware evaluation, project management for software development, and systems integration have given us an important leg up on the competition (Hopper, 1990).

Within two years of this statement being published AMR found itself at the centre of what was probably one of the most costly commercial information systems failures in history.

It is perhaps significant that AMR and AMRIS made their reputations on developing their own CRS over a long period of time, not through their involvement in a series partnership ventures. In fact, the role of AMRIS acting as both a partner and prime developer within the Intrico partnership may have contributed to problems with the Confirm project. The structure of the partnership apparently gave the Intrico Board rather than AMRIS final authority over the project. This position would have been likely to have created a conflict of interest for AMRIS as they attempted to balance their dual roles of developer and client.

The out-of-court settlement means it is difficult to ascertain the true facts of this case and to disseminate them so that others might learn to avoid the mistakes that must have been made. Rumours, untried allegations, and sensational news stories may inspire a future work of fiction or provide the basis for some interesting tutorial-type discussions based on speculation but can do little to contribute to future 'best-practice' without an agreed version from all parties of the sequence of events.

---

[3] Much of the information in this section is from *Business Week* (1994), *Technical Computing* (1992) and *Information Week* (1992).

Lessons of the Confirm Experience

The Confirm case has been cited since it is hoped that useful lessons may be drawn from it. Neither the general observations nor the prescriptive comments made below should necessarily be taken as any reflection on the Confirm project.

Organizational

Partnerships

There are inevitably going to be tensions within any partnership agreement. One source of the problems that may arise within a software development partnership may be due to the conflicting position of a partner being both an end-user and the primary developer. Another source of problems can occur if the organizational structure results in design by committee. The benefits of this approach are few, the dangers many. One problem of such a committee approach, especially if the committee is composed of players that are competitors in other areas, is that developments are at risk of failure should members pursue their own interests at the expense of the common goal.

One lesson that can be drawn from such a situation must be the avoidance of the potential conflicts of interest that can arise if partners are to act as both the purchaser and provider of the systems under development. Even if such a dual role is operated with scrupulous integrity it is a position that is very hard to defend if problems arise.

Another lesson relates to the composition and management of partnerships. Unless a common and achievable goal is agreed upon by all partners there will be a risk that each will attempt to extract maximum benefit from the development at the expense of the rest of the group. This risk will be heightened if the partners have no natural common cause and are competitors elsewhere.

Organizational Culture

Unsubstantiated claims were made but not proved during this case about a 'fear-based' culture within AMRIS where employees were apparently discouraged from speaking their minds from fear of incurring the wrath of management. This can create a situation in which staff keep their heads down and their mouths closed, so that the last people to find out what is *really* going on are the senior managers.

This is a vital lesson. It is important not to alienate the people upon whose shoulders rests the responsibility of actually creating the system. If staff do not feel they can be open about perceived problems and issues it is very likely that this will create a looking-glass world made up of optimistic management reports and positive meetings that bears no resemblance to the real state of affairs.

One side-effect of this kind of culture is the 'Optimist Effect'[4]. This phenomenon is observed in all organizations, but may be most prevalent within fear-based cultures. It occurs when managers are more receptive to bringers of good tidings and staff who adopt an optimistic outlook on the progress of a project. Managers are so receptive to these individuals that they promote them, thus building an optimistic outlook into the system. As reports pass up the chain of management the optimistic outlook can be reinforced to such an extent that the most senior management have little idea what is happening at grass-roots level. A classic example of the effects of such a regime is what happened with progress reporting in the five-year plan system in the former Soviet Union under Stalin. Ultimately the fear of failure was so great that managers simply falsified their reports in order to avoid presenting bad news to Stalin. The end result of this was that no-one, least of all Stalin himself, knew what the true state of affairs really were. However, it must be said that most managers of software development projects usually bear little resemblance to Stalin.

Staffing

A more mundane but equally important lesson relates to the problems of staff turnover. The fact that one of the partners in this case raise staff morale as an issue gives me the excuse to make a point about the sort of staffing problems that might arise. If there was indeed a high rate of staff turnover this would present management with a huge problem in recruiting, inducting, and possibly training a large number of new staff. In addition, on a large project staff may take many weeks to make an

_____ . . . .

[4] I am indebted to Tom Davis of Silicon Graphics who introduced this concept in Risks 15.80 while discussing the problems that can occur with large software development projects.

effective contribution and months to become truly conversant with the complexity of the issues surrounding their part of the development. Staff turnover, as may occur in unhappy organizations, will simply exacerbate these problems. These twin problems are well known within the industry and Fred Brooks (1982) commented:

> ... When schedule slippage is recognized, the natural (and traditional) response is to add manpower. Like dousing a fire with gasoline, this makes matters worse, much worse. More fire requires more gasoline, and thus begins a regenerative cycle which ends in disaster.

On the problem of staff turnover he was later to write:

> Not only technical problems but management problems as well come from the complexity [of information systems]. ... It makes it hard to find and control all the loose ends. It creates the tremendous learning and understanding burden that makes personnel turnover a disaster (Brooks, 1987, p.11).

The lesson from this is simple, by looking after the project team staff turnover can be kept to manageable levels. This is not only cheaper for the organization as a whole, it will also probably reduce the problems associated with project slippage.

Human Factors

The cover-up tendency

When things are going badly it is often hard to admit to oneself, let alone anyone else, the horrible truth. It is a simple psychological reality that, for most people, admitting mistakes is very difficult. If this fact is combined with the fear of severe career penalties for failure and the eternal hope that 'something will turn up', it becomes easier to understand how mistakes and oversights can be covered up. Once this process starts, however, it is then simply a matter of time before the knock-on effects of the initial concealment have themselves to be covered up. Things can then go from bad to worse.

Once initiated, and given enough time to incubate, a cover-up can proceed from the individual to the departmental, the divisional and ultimately to the corporate level (the case of the former Soviet Union under Stalin was a rare example of a national cover-up that permeated all official statistics). If, as was claimed by some, there was a cover-up within the Confirm project, and the evidence on this is by no means conclusive, it is easy to understand how, with so much at stake for all involved, it could have happened.

The lesson relates to creating effective reporting structures with the ability to drill-down to examine the fine detail of a project's progress. Part of this structure should include individuals external to the project who act as auditors of its progress. Consultants may be used for this task. However, as any text on project management will tell you, it is important both to read *and* take action on their reports.

Technical

How to assess competency?

It seems that a contributory factor to the failure of the Confirm project could have been a series of poor decisions relating to system design and the use of technology. Once staff have been employed and have begun to be deeply involved in a development, problems of this sort are very difficult to deal with. The key to problems of this sort lies partly in recruitment and selection of staff, and partly in the audit of work at important stages in a project's lifecycle.

Employing staff is often a tricky business at the best of times, employing technical staff can be an order of magnitude more complex. Ultimately, no amount of apparently impressive experience on an application form is enough, staff have to demonstrate that they can perform at the required standard over a period of time. The role of technical audit is thus very important, both for individuals and for the system as a whole.

Assessing organizational competency is also a difficult challenge. If a project is to involve an industry giant (with a reputation to match) whether as a partner like AMR or as a consultant or supplier then it almost seems to be an irrelevance. However, as we have seen, this is not the case. The question is not just 'What have you done?' but 'What have you done recently?' and 'How does this experience relate to my needs?' as well as 'How experienced are the staff to be used on this project?' In all things, reputation is not enough, a detailed demonstration of appropriate capability is required.

———————············

VARIATIONS ON A THEME

The Confirm project is an example of just how difficult it can be for succesful organizations to carry that success with them into new ventures. The case below is another example where the use of Sabre's technology did not guarantee an outright success.

SNCF and the Socrates Reservation System[5]

The French railway system, SNCF, is world famous for its advanced high-speed TGV trains and the excellence of its engineering. But its mishandling of the introduction the Socrates computerized reservation system (CRS) demonstrated how even technologically sophisticated organizations like SNCF can make elementary mistakes.

From the outset the Socrates CRS was intended to bring train ticketing into the twentieth century and provide a means of maximizing the revenue that could be obtained from the TGV network. SNCF estimated that the number of travel reservations would rise from 50 million in 1992 to 150 million in 1995, and on this basis made the decision to create a reservation system that would be able to handle the expected increase in volumes, something like AA's SABRE. Since the inspiration for Socrates was SABRE, it was fitting that AA was to be closely involved in the creation of this revolutionary system. The contract, signed in March 1989, was essentially to buy-in and modify the SABRE system to handle train rather than airline reservations. The total cost of creating the Socrates CRS, to be operational by the spring of 1993, was to be FFr1.3 billion (£140 million, $210 million).

The decision to modify the SABRE system and adopt its pricing mechanisms carried huge cultural implications for the nature of train travel in France. One of the major benefits of the SABRE system is its

——————········

[5] Much of the detail in this case study is drawn from *Le Monde Informatique* (1993), *Reuters* (1993a,b), *The Times* (1993) and *Capital* (1993).

ability to maximize the amount of revenue that may be obtained by varying the price charged according to a range of factors, including the distance you travel, where you sit, how you travel, and whether you book in advance. What is now accepted practice in air travel represented a novel idea for train travellers whose ticket price was far less variable, with the result that SNCF was intending to impose airline-style pricing practices into train travel. Like SABRE, Socrates would be demand-driven, allocating seats and choosing fares automatically. The CRS would be designed to identify peaks of demand and force prices up, thereby attempting to divert passengers to trains currently running half-empty and maximizing revenue for SNCF. Given the controversial political and commercial implications of such a change, the early planning was carried out in secret, and it was only after two years of work (and with the contract with AA safely signed) that plans for the new system were officially shown to the railway consumers associations. It was not until 1991 that the travel agents, who at that time accounted for 20% of main line ticket sales and 40% of first-class tickets, were approached—by which time much of the software was complete and changes very difficult to make.

The deadline for the introduction of Socrates was set by the head of SNCF so that it could be up and running in time for the new TGV Nord service, intended to be operational in May 1993. In November 1992 pilot runs of the new Socrates CRS in twelve stations revealed a large number of bugs in the system and culminated with the staff at Rennes station going on strike. Despite these early problems, the introduction of the new Socrates system was phased-in from the start of 1993, with over 70% of stations having been equipped with the new reservations system by February.

As the system went live the travelling public faced a large number of bizarre problems ranging from long delays of up to 45 minutes in obtaining tickets, denying the existence of the cathedral town of Rouen, to setting wildly improbable prices. High-speed trains flashed across the French countryside with just a few people on board because Socrates had falsely shown the train to be full. Even the name of the new reservation system became a liability since Socrates, the Greek philosopher, is famous for saying 'I know nothing except the fact of my ignorance'. Indeed, the system name was perhaps itself a poor choice since it was associated with philosophy, and few people view philosophy as synonymous with simplicity and clarity.

The simple task of buying a train ticket became a nightmare. The graffiti on a poster in Lille station read 'More than one hour to buy a ticket'. Part of the problems might have been due to the fact that SNCF's 6500 ticket sellers found it hard to adapt and held token strikes over the increased workload. Those travellers who gave up trying to buy a ticket before boarding their train and went on without one were liable to be fined. Chaos reigned. In an attempt to avoid the total paralysis of the TGV network SNCF suspended the requirement that all passengers must buy their ticket before travelling, permitting them instead to buy tickets from conductors once on board. This concession merely served to complicate an already difficult situation. One result of the Socrates fiasco was that the travelling public deserted the TGVs in their droves, with passenger traffic in the first nine months of 1993 falling by nearly 9%.

A government report published in July found that the public had suffered a loss in confidence in SNCF and that 50% of passengers believed that buying a ticket had become more complicated. It also went on to state that the introduction of Socrates had suffered from a lack of capital and a lack of proper training for the workers who would use it. Other problems included the use of old timetable information containing errors that were carried forward into the new data files and inadequate testing of the system before it went live. SNCF had also underestimated the time and training ticket sellers would need in order to make effective use of the system. More fundamentally, the design of Socrates was over-complex with the result that even simple journeys— that would not previously have required a reservation—became a major undertaking. Indeed, the SNCF's combination of 150 000 routes made for a complicated system with a huge number of codes.

In addition to these problems SNCF was a technical organization with an engineering focus. In the words of one consultant:

> At the top are the engineers who make all the decisions and at the bottom are the troops who don't have a say in the matter. This is the way SNCF is run.

The communications with the travelling public had also been inadequate and the travellers who would actually use the trains were not adequately prepared for the tremendous change that was to take effect. The words of Serge Sacalais, Montparnasse station chief encapsulate the problem:

> Railways are technical things filled with mostly technical people. But it's true we sort of put our foot in it because we didn't know how to communicate.

References

Brooks, F., *The Mythical Man-Month: Essays on Software Engineering*, Addison-Wesley, reading, MA (1982).

Brooks, F., 'No silver bullet: essence and accidents of software engineering', *Computer*, April, 11 (1987).

Business Week, 'Portrait of a project as a total disaster', 17 January (1994).

Capital, 'SNCF: histoire d'une modernisation ratée', May (1993).

Computerworld, 'Confirm system on schedule but future questioned', 28 May, 10 (1990).

Copeland, D. G. and McKenney, J. L., 'The airline reservation system: lessons from history', *MIS Quarterly*, September (1988).

Hopper, M. D., 'Rattling SABRE—new ways to compete on information', *Harvard Business Review*, May–June, 118–25 (1990).

InformationWeek, 'The collapse of Confirm', 12 October, (1992).

Le Monde Informatique, 'Socrate: un problème d'orchestration', 17 September (1993).

Reuters, 'French railways' booking system is a ticket to frustration', 21 July (1993a).

Reuters, 'France: unpopular Socrates forces French to rethink their rail philosophy', 23 October (1993b).

Technical Computing, 'AMR sues partners. Mainframes won't co-ordinate', 1 November (1992).

The Times, 'Socrates maddens land of Descartes', 7 September (1993).

4

THE LONDON AMBULANCE SERVICE

Computerized despatch system

. . . .

Every mistake in the book?[1]

———········

[1] This is taken from a comment made by Paul Williams of BDO Binder Hamlyn, part of the team who undertook the official inquiry into the LAS disaster, during a press conference marking the publication of the official report. When asked whether the LAS had made just about every mistake possible, he replied 'They probably went through every one in the book, yes'. Quoted in Mullin (1993).

Chronology of Major Events

1987	First computerization project commences with £3 million budget.
	Only voice transmission to ambulances included in original specification
1989	Specification amended to include transmission of data as well as voice
1990	Project abandoned at recommendation of consultants Arthur Andersen. Cost of abandonment put at £7.5 million
	Long-running industrial dispute over pay ends
1990–91	New senior management team appointed
Feb. 1991	System Requirements Specification for new Computer Aided Despatch system completed
April 1991	Major management restructuring completed
	Management slimmed by 20%
	LAS reduced from four to three Divisions
May 1991	Contractors to build system selected
June/July 1991	System Design Specification prepared
Oct. 1991	New System Manager joins LAS
Dec. 1991	Project Team recognize that original January 1992 deadline would not be met
Jan. 1992	Partial system goes live
Jan.–Sep. 1992	Despatch system implemented piecemeal across LAS Divisions
April 1992	LAS Board presented with a formal vote of no confidence in system by staff in NE Division
Oct. 1992	Central Ambulance Control reorganized
	26 Oct.—System goes live
	27 Oct.—System closed down
	28 Oct.—Reverts to semi-manual operation
	Chief Executive of LAS resigns
	External Enquiry announced by Health Secretary
Nov. 1992	System crashes, fallback routines fail to operate
	System closed down
	Revert to entirely manual operation
Feb. 1993	Inquiry Report published
	Chairman of LAS resigns

The collapse of the new mission-critical LAS ambulance despatch system after less than two days of operation was widely reported and was one of the most dramatic computer failures of recent years. The official government inquiry into the disaster ensured that it was also one of the best documented. This case provides an in-depth examination of the circumstances surrounding the development and subsequent failure of the system that was intended to be a 'quantum leap' in technology. The causes of the failure are analysed in detail and a range of important lessons drawn relating to many aspects of the systems development process. The detailed information in this case, except when otherwise referenced, comes from Page *et al.* (1993).

Introduction

The London Ambulance Service (LAS) is the largest ambulance service in the world. The LAS provides ambulance cover for a major capital city and is responsible for a geographical area of 600 square miles and a resident population of nearly 7 million people. During the working day the population increases dramatically as millions of commuters head for Central London and the City. This level of population inevitably generates a heavy load on the emergency services, and on a typical day the LAS will carry over 5000 patients and receive between 2000 and 2500 calls, of which some 1600 will be related to accidents and emergencies.

The work of the LAS can be divided into the Accident and Emergency Service (A&E) and Patient Transport Service (PTS). The scale of the LAS operation is huge. Typically, its fleet of 300+ A&E ambulances will make around 500000 patient journeys in a year, with 400+ PTS ambulances making a further 1.3 million patient journeys.

The LAS was founded in 1930, the service having previously been run by the Metropolitan Asylum Board. Since 1974 the LAS has been part of the National Health Service (NHS) and had been managed by South West Thames Regional Health Authority since that time. It employed around 2700 staff and for the financial year 1992/3 its budgeted income was £69.7 million.

The Computer Aided Despatch Development

One of the major responsibilities of the LAS is responding to calls to attend accidents and emergencies. The LAS will typically receive over 1500 emergency calls a day, with each call being screened before an ambulance is despatched to the incident.

The manual resource allocation (ambulance despatch) system that was used by the LAS prior to the 1992 changeover is depicted in Figure 4.1. The process of receiving a call and despatching an ambulance, which from start to finish (according to UK performance standards for ambulance services) should take no more than 3 minutes, operates as follows:

1. An emergency call is received by Central Ambulance Control.
2. A control assistant writes down the details of the incident on a form, identifies its location from a map book, and determines the map reference.
3. The incident form is placed onto a conveyor belt to take it, and all the forms relating to other incidents, to a central collection point.
4 The forms are received at the central collection point and passed to one of three resource allocators (one for each of the London Divisions—North East, North West, and South), with possible duplicate calls being identified.
5. Using information on the current status and location of each ambulance (gained from the radio operator and the activity form on each vehicle), the resource allocator decides which resource (paramedic, helicopter, ambulance, etc.) to mobilize. This is recorded on the incident form and passed on to a despatcher.
6. Finally, the despatcher either telephones the appropriate ambulance station or passes mobilization instructions to a radio operator if the ambulance is out of the station.

The problems of operating a manual paper-based system in such a high-pressure situation in which there is no control over the volume of incoming calls were well understood throughout the LAS. Particular problems included:

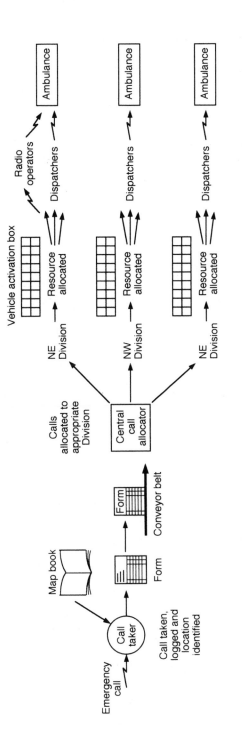

Figure 4.1 Central Ambulance Control

- The sometimes slow identification of the precise location of incidents due to incomplete or inaccurate details from the caller
- The cumbersome use of paper throughout the system
- The need to rely on sometimes fallible human judgement to identify duplicate calls
- Communication bottlenecks and mobilization queues due to the slow process of contacting ambulances.

The impact of the limitations of the manual ambulance despatch system was that performance standards were much lower than the nationally agreed standards for ambulance response. The introduction of a computer-aided despatch system was thus viewed as a highly attractive means of improving performance levels within the LAS.

With the background of a creaking manual system and a recently abandoned computerization project (that failed partly as a result of being unable to cope with changing requirements), the decision was made to create a new command and control system that would be a technological leap ahead of anything else that existed.

The primary aim of the new system was to create an efficient streamlined command and control system to enable appropriate resources to be despatched with the minimum of delay. This was to be realized by designing out of the new system the need for human intervention in handling the majority of resource allocations, with human operators being required for only the most complex situations. The role of the redesignated call assistants would now be to receive incoming calls, enter them into the system, and see each incident through to completion. The system would then automatically determine in which of the three Divisions the incident was located, eliminate duplicate calls, and then identify and despatch the most appropriate resource.

The new system would automate away many of the problems associated with the existing manual system by incorporating a range of features that would include:

- Computerized map system with public call box identification
- Vehicle location tracking
- Automatic update of resource availability
- Automatic identification of duplicate calls
- Automatic ambulance mobilization (in simple cases)

At the time this was being planned some organizations had successfully implemented either computerized call taking or vehicle location mapping and were examining automatic ambulance mobilization. What was innovative about this proposal was that no other organization in the UK, certainly no other emergency service, had attempted to combine computerized call taking, vehicle location mapping and automatic resource allocation in a single system. What was even more ambitious, from a technical point of view, was the decision to move in one stage, termed a 'Quantum Leap', from an entirely manual to a totally automated system.

The decision to build a bespoke system was based partly on the view that the scale of the LAS operation, and the nature of London as a modern city and seat of government, presented a combination of unique requirements. An attempt was made at the end of 1990 to examine several existing computerized despatch systems, but all were rejected on cost or other grounds.

The creation of a totally automated system was also seen by management as very attractive since it could potentially have an impact on several difficult problems:

- Poor industrial relations
- What were perceived as outmoded working practices by ambulance crews, including the ability of the crews or stations themselves to decide which ambulance to send to an incident
- The absence of reliable information on LAS resource requirements. Once accurate information became available the impression that resources were not being used to best effect could be examined and used to support higher funding or to make changes to staff working patterns.

The context into which the new system was to be introduced was far from ideal. However, while it can be argued that there is never an ideal time to introduce a major new computer system, seldom can such a major information systems development have been attempted in such challenging circumstances.

In order to appreciate just how challenging these circumstances were, it is necessary to take a short look at each of the major factors that were impacting on the LAS around the time of the ambulance despatch project.

Systems development in the LAS has a troubled past. The first attempt to introduce the Computer Aided Despatch (CAD) of ambulances began in the early 1980s with a radio-based voice system. In 1987, after some delays, the £3 million ($4.5 million) project commenced, only to have its specification changed in 1989 to include the transmission of data as well as voice to ambulances. The project was abandoned in October 1990, at a cost of £7.5 million ($11.25 million), after system load tests revealed that it would probably not be able to cope with anticipated levels of demand.

In February 1991 LAS initiated proceedings to seek damages from the suppliers of the failed system, a prospect complicated by the changes made to the original specification two years after it had commenced. A settlement was later reached.

It was perhaps little comfort to the LAS that it was not the only ambulance service in the UK having difficulties developing computer systems. A report published in 1990 by the National Audit Office revealed that of the 62 ambulance services in the UK, 25 had either not attempted or abandoned attempts to computerize route scheduling activities.

At the end of the 1980s the UK government had embarked on a total reorganization of the NHS with the aim of introducing an internal market in healthcare. This involved major upheavals in the way in which healthcare was both purchased and provided. Prior to the creation of the internal market in healthcare the National Health Service (NHS) provided seamless links between those needing healthcare services, the patients, and those providing them, the hospitals. The changes introduced to the NHS effectively split healthcare into two groups—purchasers (doctors or Health Authorities) and providers (the hospitals and other organizations used to treat patients). Under this new system local doctors or Regional Health Authorities (acting on behalf of patients) were able to 'buy' treatments from hospitals. This created an 'internal market' in which hospitals would bid against each other to supply treatment services. The aim of this major change in the structure and ethos of the NHS was to make the whole system more efficient.

The immediate implications for the LAS of this change involved profound alterations in management practice, with managers facing the prospect of having to bid in a highly competitive market to provide patient transport services for some 80 hospitals and community units, something that had not been required before.

By the beginning of the 1990s, due to the changes taking place within the NHS, the management of the LAS was facing a period of enforced restructuring . Between 1990 and 1991, following the creation of a new management framework, a new senior management team consisting of a Chief Executive and Directors of Operations, Human Resources and Finance were appointed. By April 1991 this new team had completed a major management restructuring exercise that had reduced senior and middle management posts by nearly 20%.

This restructuring resulted in a large number of experienced staff leaving the organization and the reported creation of a great deal of stress among those managers that remained. Much of the stress associated with this restructuring was, it is said (NUPE Submission, 1992, pp. 24–6), due to the absence of any consultation over the changed management structure or the new job descriptions within which managers would have to work.

This reorganization took place at the end of a period that was characterized by a lack of investment across the whole of the LAS and, in particular, a period during which there had been little or no investment in management training and development. The result of this lack of investment was reported to be a managerial style that was inward-looking and old-fashioned.

The year 1990 saw the end of a hard-fought national industrial dispute over pay and conditions that had left relations between managers and staff strained. A legacy of this dispute was that LAS management perceived the trade unions as obstructive and resistant to change, while the trade unions believed that management were attempting to marginalize them and undermine their position.

Performance standards for ambulance services were laid down by the government in 1974. These standards provide guidelines both for the time it should take for an ambulance to be 'activated' once a call has been received and, once activated, how long it should take to arrive at the scene. These standards (as they related to the LAS) are shown below:

Activation time
95% of all calls should result in an ambulance being 'activated' within 3 minutes

Response time

50% of all Ambulance calls should result in an ambulance 'on scene' within 8 minutes

95% of all ambulance calls should result in an ambulance 'on scene' within 14 minutes

According to the NUPE Submission to the official inquiry (pp. 10–11) the LAS had not met these standards of performance for some time.

System Specification and Supplier Selection

The development of the systems requirements specification (SRS) for the proposed new system was overseen by a project committee that included the Systems Manager, a systems analyst working on contract and the Control Room Services Manager, and was chaired by the Director of Support Services. Although (through union representatives) ambulance crews were invited to join the committee, there was little involvement at this stage due to problems surrounding the staff consultation process. In the event it was reported (Page *et al.*, 1993, p. 20) that the majority of the work was done by the contract analyst and Systems Manager, with the Systems Requirement specification being completed in February 1991. There was no formal sign-off of the completed specification.

The implications for staff working practices of the newly completed specification were profound and were contained in new guidelines published at the same time. However, there was little involvement from the ambulance crews themselves in the design of these new working practices.

The new computer aided despatch system was designed from the start to make use of some of the components of the system that was abandoned in 1990. The structure of the proposed new system is illustrated in Figure 4.2. Of the five following major components of the new system

1. Computer Aided Despatch system
2. Computer Map Display system
3. Automatic Vehicle Location System (ALVS)
4. Mobile Data Terminals (MDT)
5. Radio Interface System (RIFS)

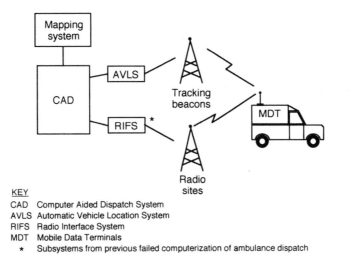

KEY
CAD   Computer Aided Dispatch System
AVLS Automatic Vehicle Location System
RIFS Radio Interface System
MDT   Mobile Data Terminals
  *   Subsystems from previous failed computerization of ambulance dispatch

Figure 4.2 Structure of the LAS computerized despatch system. CAD—Computer Aided Despatch system, AVLS—Automatic Vehicle Location System, RIFS—Radio Interface System, MDT—Mobile Data Terminals. *Sub-system from previous failed computerization of ambulance despatch

both the Mobile Data Terminals and the Radio Interface System installed as part of the previously aborted system were to be re-used.

The functionality of this new system was not only far greater than the previously failed system, but was also greater than was available from any other existing computerized ambulance despatch system.

The process of finding an organization or consortium to build the new system began with the creation of a small selection team. An advertisement on 7 February 1991 attracted interest from 35 companies, of whom 17 were to bid for contracts to supply all or part of the new system. An issue that came up repeatedly in the discussions between the LAS and the potential suppliers was the tightness of the proposed timetable. All were told that full implementation should take place by the non-negotiable date of 8 January 1992.

In assessing the 17 proposals that had been received the selection team used a system of awarding points against a checklist of features. The main features used to assess each bid are shown below in order of their importance:

1. Ability to perform the tasks required
2. Ability to handle throughput and response times
3. Ease of use by staff
4. Resilience
5. Flexibility
6. Ability to meet timetable
7. Cost
8. Additional features.

In addition to the inflexibility of the deadline it was also believed by senior LAS managers that the system could be built at a cost of around £1.5 million ($2.25 million).[2] At any event, given the strict financial guidelines that governed the purchasing process, the LAS were obliged to accept the lowest tender unless they had 'good and sufficient reasons to the contrary'. The selection team recommended that the lowest tender be accepted.

The winning proposal was produced by a consortium of Apricot (a UK hardware supplier owned by Mitsubishi), Systems Options (a small software house), and Datatrak (who would supply the vehicle location systems). The proposal, which contained far more detail on the hardware rather than the software to be used within the system, indicated that the cost of developing the computer aided despatch software would be less than 4% of the overall amount. This amount was significantly lower than any of the other proposals. The winning Apricot/Systems Options/ Datatrak price of just under £1 million ($1.5 million), was less than one-third the price of some of the highest bids, with the next lowest bid being £700 000 ($1.05 million) more expensive.

The Apricot bid was significantly lower than the other tenders that had been received. However, the issue of why the software cost was so low was not pursued. Although supplier references were taken up in the normal manner, there was no systematic inquiry into the competence of any of the suppliers. Of the supplier references that were received, two referred to the extent to which the resources of Systems Options were

—————·.......

[2] It is unclear where the figure of £1.5 million came from. However, an earlier report by Arthur Andersen (to advise on future action after the previous IS failure) stated that if a packaged solution could be found a budget of £1.5 million would be appropriate. It went on to say that this estimate should be significantly increased if a suitable package was not available.

already heavily committed. Of the three members of the consortium it was agreed with the LAS that Systems Options, a small software house, would be the lead contractor.

Prior to the recommendation being passed to the Board of the LAS the papers were sent to another ambulance service for an impartial examination of the selection process. The report endorsed the supplier selection but noted that:

> The LAS management should ... satisfy themselves that the decision to choose a system which will be specially written is preferred to choosing an existing one. ... This is a fundamental decision which requires management's explicit endorsement.

The external assessor made no reference to the widely differing prices contained within the tenders received.

The final decision to approve the supplier recommendation was taken by the Board of the LAS. The minutes of the meeting contain no evidence that there was any discussion about the wide range of the bids received or that the winning bid was significantly lower than any other. There is also no evidence that the issues raised by the external assessor of the selection process were discussed.

System Design and Build

The concept behind the LAS Computer Aided Despatch system was to automate, as far as was possible, the existing manual system of resource allocation. The structure of the new system was to be made up of the elements shown in Figure 4.3 and would operate as follows:

1. Call is received by the Control Assistant.
2. Control Assistant takes details from the caller and enters them into the Computer Aided Despatch (CAD) system.
3. The location of the incident is pinpointed using a combination of mapping system and call-box identifier.
4. Using the incident information received the CAD system then informs Control Assistant the level of the emergency (on a scale of 1–10) and advises which skills and special vehicles should be used.
5. Using information received on the current location and status of ambulances (obtained from the vehicle tracking system and mobile

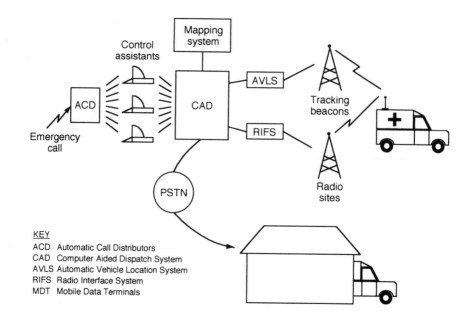

Figure 4.3 Structure of the new CAD system. ACD—Automatic Call Distributor. For other abbreviations see Figure 4.2

data terminals), the level of the emergency, and the location of the incident, a rule-based system is used to identify the closest appropriate vehicle.

6. Control Assistants then allocate indicated resources, and the CAD system sends a mobilization signal and incident details.

7. As the ambulance crew deal with the incident they press different buttons on the mobile data terminal to update the CAD system of their changing status. First, one button is pressed to acknowledge the call, a second when they arrive at the scene of the incident, a third when they leave the scene, a fourth when they arrive at the hospital, and a fifth when they are free to take another call. This information, together with data from the Automatic Vehicle Location System (AVLS), is used to update the CAD system so that it knows the status and location of all resources at any point in time.

The new CAD system would thus transform what had been an intensely manual approach relying upon human interaction and trust into an impartial automated system that takes the majority of the decision making away from the staff.

While many command and control systems of this type are usually based on minicomputers, the LAS system was designed to run over a network with three file servers, two of which were to be used as backups. The CAD system was designed to operate in a client–server mode with the majority of processing taking place on (for the time) powerful 25 MHz Intel 486-based Apricot workstations.

The core of the system is the software that decides which available resource should be allocated to attend a particular incident. This processor-intensive activity is handled by the workstations, with the program code being written in the high-level C programming language. A feature of the system is that the time taken to deal with resource requests increases, the greater the distance between an incident and potential resources. This is due to the complexity of the time and distance calculations that must be done in order to identify the most appropriate resource. The system would thus inevitably slow down at busy times when the number of incidents rises and there are fewer resources not already dealing with a call.

At an early stage it was decided that there would be a trade-off between ease of use and performance to enable the system to have a user-friendly interface, with Microsoft Windows 3.0 being selected. Although not specified in the original Apricot/Systems Options/Datatrak proposal (because it had not at that time been released), the Visual Basic (v1) development tool was used to create the screen dialogues.

The situation in May 1991, after the contract was awarded to the Apricot/Systems options/Datatrak consortium, was that the components of the system would be supplied as follows:

	System component	*Responsibilities*
Systems Options	Computer Aided Despatch (CAD) software	Project leader Systems Integrator Produce System Design Spec.
Apricot	CAD hardware	
Datatrak	Automatic vehicle location system (AVLS)	
SOLO	Mobile data terminals (MDT) Radio Interface software (RIFS)	

The contract, awarded in May 1991, stipulated that this entire system was to be developed, tested and implemented in a single phase by 8 January 1992, a project duration of a little over six months. During the months of June and July 1991 Systems Options prepared a full Systems Design Specification (SDS), but it was not until September 1991 that the contract with SOLO was signed.

The PRINCE (Project In Controlled Environment, a UK government standard) project management methodology was to be used throughout the development. However, since neither the suppliers nor the staff in the LAS had any direct experience of using this methodology, a course was run for the principal team members to give them some knowledge of PRINCE.

A project group meeting in June 1991 raised a number of potential concerns about the development, including:

- The LAS had no staff assigned full-time to the project
- The lack of clarification of how PRINCE was to be applied to the project
- The lack of a formal programme for project group and other meetings
- The fact that the time scale of six months was rather less than the industry average (around 18 months) for a project of this type
- The draft project plan provided by the supplier left no time for review and revision.

There is no evidence that any further action was taken on any of the concerns raised at this meeting.

Despite the original intention that the new system be supplied on a turnkey basis, with suppliers taking responsibility for all aspects of its development and implementation, this intention was not written into the contract. Although Systems Options were to be the project managers, this role seems to have been performed by the contract analyst and the Director of Support Services in addition to their normal duties.

In order to manage the problems that would arise in software or hardware during the development a Project Issue Report (PIR) system was established. This ensured that identified problems would remain visible, and that changes made to correct the system were documented. When issued a Project Issue Report would be allocated a status between 1 and 4 according to the seriousness of the problem.

The intention of this system was to enable those running the project to have some level of control over the identification, and subsequent resolution, of systems development problems. Although throughout its operation some 1513 PIRs were raised, this represented only a partial record of development problems.

In October 1991 a new Systems Manager joined the LAS and, although he was not asked to take over the project, he conducted independent reviews of its progress in November 1991 and March 1992. In the second of these reports, as a result of doubts about the error control system, he recommended that control of the PIR system should be with the project team (and not Systems Options), and that all changes should be agreed within this system.

In the early stages of the development process, after a proposal had been made by another consultancy firm[3] to undertake software Quality Assurance (QA), the project team made the decision to allow Systems Options to handle their own QA and thus avoid the additional costs involved.

Staff Changes and Training

In January 1992 the LAS commissioned a staff attitude survey from Price Waterhouse. The results published three months later revealed a number of insights into staff views on the LAS, its management, and their own jobs (see NUPE, 1992, pp. 34–5):

On the LAS
- 13% of staff believe the LAS provide a 'quality service'
- 10% of staff felt that they knew what the LAS plans were for the future

On the LAS management
- 24% of staff felt that senior management were committed to quality
- 11% of all staff believed that management dealt with mistakes in an open manner

————········

[3] The consultancy ISL—originally working with one of the organizations who failed to win the contract.

- 8% of all staff believed that management listened to them and helped implement their ideas
- 68% of staff feel they do not get any feedback from management
- 26% of staff felt that their 'boss' keeps them informed

On their own job

- 66% of all staff were not satisfied with their job
- 65% of staff believed that they do not receive recognition for the job they do

An earlier survey by ACAS (Arbitration Conciliation and Advisory Service) into occupational stress published in 1989 also made a number of observations that provide an insight into the LAS at that time (NUPE Submission, 1992, pp. 25–6):

> A large majority of interviewees felt that increasingly management did not have the time or sometimes the skills to deal with staff as human beings. ... Staff generally felt that the Service was moving from one where caring for its employees was moving from a high to a low priority.
> The great majority of staff felt the Service was deteriorating and that pressures at work were increasing.
> Staff generally viewed both the quantity and quality of workplace communications in the LAS as inadequate.
> The management style was perceived by staff to be bureaucratic and uncaring.

ACAS found that staff experienced

> problems in a number of organizational areas including management style, communications, training and discipline. ... [These] led to many pressures..., some minor but all usually on-going and relentless, being placed on staff which gradually wore them down.

The new Computer Aided Despatch system was being developed against a background of poor labour relations, a lack of trust between staff and management, low staff morale, and enforced reorganization. The appointment of a new Chief Executive Officer of the LAS in 1990 was seen by staff representatives as being indicative of the changes ahead:

> [He] had a reputation as a tough operator within the ambulance
> service. Staff believe that he was chosen by the RHA [Regional
> Health Authority] for this very reason. Firstly they wanted to wash
> their hands of a troublesome and time consuming service and
> therefore wanted someone who would support the management of
> the LAS as a quasi-autonomous arms-length service. Secondly they
> wanted someone who would 'sort-out' the staff as they believed
> that obstructive and interfering trade unions were the basic
> problem of the service (NUPE, Submission, 1992, p. 4).

The introduction of the new Computer Aided Despatch system seems
to have been seen by management as a kind of panacea or cure-all for
the problems the LAS faced, in that the new system would not only
reduce the effect of the continual industrial relations problems but
would also eliminate a range of working practices perceived by the
management as being inefficient. The new system was designed to work
in an entirely impartial way by identifying and despatching the most
suitable resource according to a set of predefined rules. The introduction
of the new computerized system should thus no longer make it possible
for ambulance crews to make their own decisions as to which
ambulance they should take, or the local stations to decide which crews
should be sent to an incident.

The new system would also greatly increase the pressure on the
Control Assistants. In the old manual system Control Assistants recorded
an incident before passing it on to an allocator who would then identify
the optimum resource to despatch. The new system, however, would
require the Control Assistant to be solely responsible for entering the
information that the system would use to decide which resource to
send.

The introduction of the new system was intended to automate away
the inefficient aspects of the old manual system, with its handwritten
incident record forms, allocation boxes and reliance upon the use of
voice-based radio or telephone mobilization. This was to be a major
change in working practice for all staff, yet there was little consultation
with ambulance staff on the changed working practices that it required.

For the ambulance crews the system was intended to reduce local
decision making about which vehicle or crew should be used and be

impartial in its allocations. One of the implications of the new system was that, since it would always automatically allocate the nearest available resource, ambulance crews could no longer rely upon operating in familiar areas close to their home station. Instead, the impartial allocation system meant that crews would often be asked to attend incidents out of their patch, and then be given additional jobs that were at an ever-increasing distance from their home base. This meant not only that crews were operating in areas they did not know but also that they would be likely to face a long drive in heavy traffic to return to their base at the end of a shift.

The move from the voice-based method of despatching ambulances to one that relied upon computer communications eliminated the important element of personal contact that existed between staff in Central Ambulance Control and the ambulance crews. The impersonal computer-based nature of the new system had the effect of exacerbating already difficult staff–management relations.

Resistance to the changes being made did take place, being concentrated around the misuse of the Automatic Vehicle Location System (AVLS) and the Mobile Data Terminals (MBTs). However Datatrak, the primary contractor for the vehicle location sub-system, stated that resistance at LAS was no greater than that experienced by them at other organizations (Page *et al;*, 1993, p. 30). Overall, staff resistance to the new system was slight and did not represent a significant problem to the operation of the system as a whole.

Staff training was provided by a combination of Systems Options staff and LAS Work Based Trainers, and was designed to be completed by the original implementation date of 8 January 1992. Staff representatives protested over inadequate training at a meeting shortly after this date, stating that Central Ambulance Control staff had received just two days' general training to familiarise themselves with the system (NUPE Submission, 1992, p. 38). However, the long delay experienced before the system was finally to be implemented, and the continual changes being made to it during development, made it virtually impossible to achieve consistent and comprehensive training.

The training plan provided for the two staff groups who would be operating the system, the Central Control Room staff and the Ambulance staff, to be trained separately.

System Testing

A thorough testing strategy that has been completed before implementation is a key element in any systems development. In a development as complex and leading-edge as the LAS Computer Aided Despatch system it would be sensible to ensure not only that the system operates according to specification (functional testing), and that the components can operate together (integration testing), but also that the entire system can cope with the demands expected to be placed upon it (load testing). In fact, for a safety-critical system of this type, thorough testing must form a crucial element in any development process. There is no evidence that this was done.

An important element in a system of this type, which faces a largely unpredictable and wholly uncontrollable level of demand, is its behaviour as the load increases. Performance should decline in a predictable way, and tests should seek to establish how the system reacts to a broad range of events like (in this case) rapid rises in calls, the entering of conflicting information, incidents being reported more than once, vehicle location problems, mobile data terminal problems, and general operator error. The effect of such problems on the generation and resolution of exception messages, and their effect on overall system performance, should also be tested. There are no records of any of these tests having taken place.

The first major attempt at functional and load testing was undertaken with a partial system in January 1992. With several important parts of the system still incomplete the results of this test were not of much use and, while individual component testing continued, the system was never tested in its entirety prior to implementation.

One of the key elements of the system, the relationship between the despatch sub-system and the communications sub-systems (voice, vehicle-location and mobile data terminal), was never fully tested. A memo (quoted in Page *et al.*, 1993, p. 37) from the Assistant Director of Operations to the Accident and Emergency Team sent shortly before the original implementation date of 8 January 1992: 'Following the *initial operating period of the CAD system*, a full review of the radio network capability will be carried out...' (my italics). The implication of this seems to be that live operation would form part of the testing regime.

An important part of any programme of testing is to ensure that any procedures for reverting to backup processors or servers actually work. As will be remembered, the CAD system was based on powerful work-stations connected over a LAN to three file servers, two of which were backups. While the provision of two fallback file servers (including one on a remote site) were intended to be sufficient to provide for most contingencies, by the time the entire system was finally implemented in October 1992 they had not been either fully installed or tested.

Implementation

The decision to go for full implementation of the system in a single phase was taken at an early stage of the project, a phased approach being rejected on the grounds that it would not enable improvements in service to be achieved. However, due to the inability of suppliers to meet the agreed deadline, a phased approach was later to be adopted.

The Computer Aided Despatch system was implemented in the following three phases:

- *Phase I.* The call-taking and mapping systems go live, with calls being passed to allocators who use the existing manual system (activation boxes) to identify the resource before passing the incident on for despatch by telephone or radio. This phase would be based on the three existing Divisional operations.
- *Phase II.* This phase eliminates the use of voice despatch and intro-duces vehicle tracking (using the Automatic Vehicle Location System) and mobile data terminals (MDT).

Once incidents are entered into the system they are transferred to an allocators terminal. Using the information on ambulance location and status displayed on the screen, and the information in the activation box, the allocator identifies the optimum resource and despatches it using the mobile data terminals. This phase would also be based on the three existing Divisional operations.

- *Phase III.* This phase eliminates the activation boxes and enables the CAD system to make resource allocations most of the time, with allo-cators being used for the most complex cases. It was intended that this phase would operate without paper backup and replace the Divisional operations, covering all of London. Once calls are entered this final phase automates the allocation of resources for all cases in which a resource would be expected to arrive within 11 minutes from the time of despatch. Other cases would be passed on to an allocator.

When the original deadline for full implementation was not met the project team, wishing to demonstrate that progress had been made, decided to go for a partial implementation of the system—Phase I.

Although Phase I centred around the use of printers to pass incidents on to the allocators, they were not designed to be used in this way and this caused a number of problems with the operation of the system. Problems included screens locking up, server failure, and the accidental loss of a number of calls when a printer was switched off and the contents of its buffer memory cleared. These problems did not inspire confidence in the system and shortly after the calls were lost the decision was made to revert to the previous manual system (NUPE Submission, 1992, p. 38).

Throughout the period up to October 1992 Phases I and II of the system were introduced in a piecemeal fashion across the three LAS districts. The following list below (composed of material in Page *et al*, 1993, pp. 31–3) shows some of the problems that occurred during this period:

Software-related problems
- Inability of resource proposal software to identify nearest available resource
- Failure of AVLS system to identify every 53rd vehicle in the fleet

Communications
- Overload of communications channels
- Inaccurate location information from the AVLS
- Failure of mobile data system

Hardware problems
- Locking up of workstations
- Slowness of system in operation

End-user problems
- Poor status reporting by ambulance crews
- Crews taking a different ambulance from the one allocated by the system

These problems led, in turn, to outcomes that included:

- Failure of calls to reach ambulances
- Incorrect or missing vehicle locations
- Failure to identify duplicate calls
- Calls being lost in the system
- Call waiting queues growing so fast that they scrolled off the top of the screen
- Lack of prioritisation of error messages
- Exception message queues growing so fast that they scrolled off the top of the screen
- Deterioration in service
- Loss of confidence in the efficient operation of the system.

Throughout the period leading up to the full implementation in October of 1992 the system was being constantly changed as features were trialled, known faults fixed, and various phases of the system rolled-out in one or more of the three LAS Divisions.

At no time before the full implementation in October was the system either stable or operational (at the Phase III level of completeness) across all three LAS Divisions.

Until 26 October 1992 the CAD system was being used in the hybrid Phase II mode shown in Figure 4.4 (Page et al., 1993, pp. 51–4). As can be seen, this version of the system made use of the vehicle location (AVLS) and mobile data terminal (MDT) elements, but also retained the Divisional allocators, despatchers and radio operators. This combination of automation with paper backup enabled staff to work around the known system problems, with allocators basing their decision as to the optimum resource to be used on the basis of information received from the system and the manual activation boxes.

The move to full implementation of the system, Phase III, would do away with manual backups and rely upon the CAD system to make the majority of resource allocations. This required moving from the existing Divisional structure and the adoption of a 'pan-London' approach to incident handling within a unified control room. The control room itself was to be reorganized, with similar staff types, such as resource allocators and radio operators, being grouped together in different parts of the room.

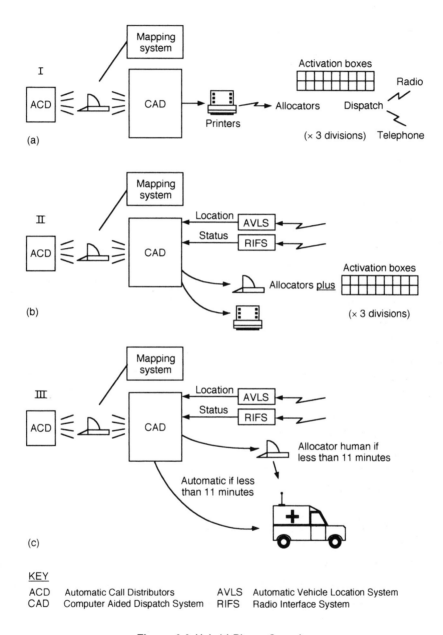

KEY

ACD	Automatic Call Distributors	AVLS	Automatic Vehicle Location System
CAD	Computer Aided Dispatch System	RIFS	Radio Interface System

Figure 4.4 Hybrid Phase 2 mode

As has been seen, staff training had been patchy and would have been of reduced effect due to changes that had been made in the system and the time lag between the date of training and implementation.

At the time of the full implementation the system was still not operating as expected and a number of problems remained, including:

- Potential for communications system to become overloaded
- Unreliability of mobile data terminals
- Unreliability of vehicle tracking
- Mapping system incomplete
- Unreliability of CAD software
- Slowness of CAD system in operation

In addition to these general problems, of the 81 Project Issue Reports (PIRs) still outstanding, two were classified as 'Severe service degradation; system will not function in the operational environment until this is rectified'. These PIRs related to problems with the incorrect decoding of status reports from MDTs (Mobile Data Terminals), and the display of multiple incident reports. The full list of outstanding PIRs is shown below:

Status	Description	No. outstanding on 26 Oct. 1992
1	System cannot be started, is unusable or cannot handle major operational situation	0
2	Severe service degradation; system will not function in the operational environment until this is rectified	2
3	Will cause problems in an operational environment resulting in poorer quality of service to patient	44
4	Minor problems requiring attention; system can be implemented with this fault, but it should be rectified beforehand if possible	35

The entire system had also not been tested to Phase 3 operation across the whole of London, and its behaviour under load was not known. The LAS did not have their own network manager and had not tested the procedures associated with fallback from the primary to the backup servers.

Throughout the entire period covering the development and implementation of the new Computer Aided Despatch system the LAS did not have a network manager, with all network housekeeping being handled by Systems Options. When network problems arose the LAS relied upon Systems Options staff to rectify the situation and, while it was always the intention of the LAS to employ its own network manager, no action had been taken prior to going live with the system.

Live Operation

At 7 a.m. on Monday 26 October the LAS Computer Aided Despatch system went live. The first problems began to show up during the morning rush when it became obvious to the ambulance crews and control room staff that things were going badly wrong. Emergency calls that had been accepted appeared to be getting 'lost' in the system causing an increasing number of duplicate calls. The rise in the number of calls led to distraught callers being held by the call-queuing system for anything up to 30 minutes before their requests were dealt with. The ambulance allocation system apparently failed to recognize the existence of certain roads with the result that staff had to revert to using a map to identify the road and a telephone to deal with ambulance despatch, causing still more delays. The result of this fatal combination was that ambulances either failed to arrive at an incident, arrived late, or turned up two at a time.

By Monday night the volume of calls and messages began to swamp the system, causing new emergency calls to overwrite earlier calls that had not been dealt with, thus leaving an increasing number of unanswered calls in the system. This caused the generation of exception messages, alerting operators that calls had not been acknowledged by ambulance crews, demanding priority action. The growing number of exception messages began to overwhelm the staff, leading to still more delays as the system slowed under the weight of uncleared exception messages. At one point, the exception report queue was cleared in an attempt to speed up the system, an action that probably increased the number of 'lost' incidents, prompting further incoming calls and adding to the spiral of delays.

By Tuesday afternoon the situation had become so bad that the system was shut down. When the operations restarted the despatchers reverted to a previously used (and mostly trusted) combination of computerized call-taking and manual allocation of ambulances. This hybrid solution, although not without problems, appeared to work well and, together with the additional call-taking staff allocated to each shift, improved call waiting times.

This situation continued for around a week until 2 a.m. on 4 November 1992 when the system slowed down and then locked up altogether. Attempts to reboot the system failed to correct the problem and, when the backup system failed to cut-in, the control room staff had no alternative but to revert to a fully manual paper-based system.

Causes of the LAS Despatch System Failure

Unfortunately there is not space here to consider in detail every single factor that contributed to the failure of the LAS Computer Aided Despatch system. In addition to examining the primary factors involved however, this section will look at the most important secondary causes. Readers will no doubt be able to contribute their own list to the secondary factors examined below.

The report of the LAS Inquiry is a remarkable document since it provides a detailed view into the many aspects of a major IS development that failed. In this it is almost unique.

Primary Causes

System design

At the heart of this disaster was the creation of a system design that was based on a perfect world where technology works as it supposed to, people do as they are told, unexpected things never happen, and problems can be designed away. While technically feasible, this approach to system design takes little account of the real world where technology is unreliable, people don't do what you want them to, the unexpected always happens, and problems don't just go away.

In the design world of the system uninterrupted feeds of data are used to update vehicle location and status information, with resources being despatched in response to calls from known locations. This is not the real world of 'lost' resources due to communications problems, of ambulance crews pressing the wrong status buttons, of duplicate calls, of unknown incident locations. Once the real world intruded into the design world, the effect could only be a spiralling decline in performance.

The collapse of the CAD system on 26 and 27 October was due to the cumulative effect of related problems that combined to produce a spiral of decline in its performance. At the heart of this decline was the absence of the near-perfect information upon which the system relied to identify the optimum resource to despatch to an incident.

As a result of the problems (Page *et al*, 1993, pp. 51–4) with vehicle tracking (AVLS) and the operation of the in-cab (MDTs) the system knew the correct location of an ever-decreasing number of ambulances and the number of exception messages began to grow rapidly. This slowed still further the system, whose performance was declining as a result of having both a dwindling number of known resources and an increasing amount of incorrect information on the location and status of ambulances. The result of this was that vehicle allocation suffered with inappropriate or multiple vehicles being despatched to incidents, and the whole process taking an ever longer time.

The operators faced a rising tide of unanswered new calls, exception messages and call-backs due to the non-appearance of ambulances, together with a declining number of resources that were known to the system. The control room staff and the ambulance crews were faced with an impossible situation and frustration as they tried for a day and a half to make the system work.

The whole situation was exacerbated by the reorganization of the central control room that had eliminated the paper-based allocation boxes and split up the Divisional teams, thus making it very difficult for staff to identify and overrule incorrect system decisions. The complex web of cause and effect that led to this spiral of decline in performance is illustrated in Figure 4.5.

The success of the system thus depended upon the faultless operation and interaction of all its major component parts. However, the central problem, as identified by the Inquiry Report, was that:

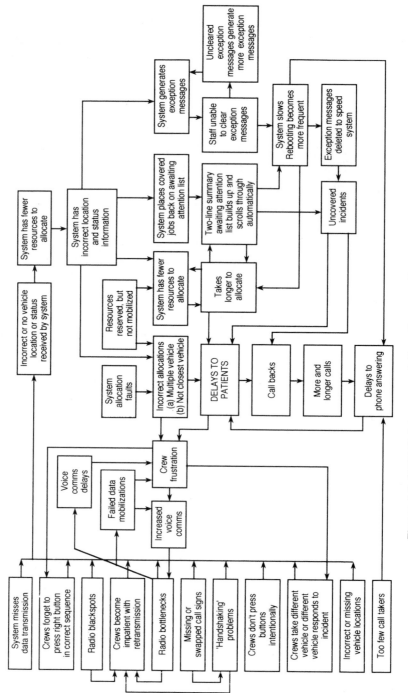

Figure 4.5 26/27 October cause/effect diagram. (Source: Page et al., 1993)

it is probable that the development team did not have a full appreciation of the importance of these elements or, at least, of the consequences of failure, or less than perfect performance, of any one part (Page *et al;*, 1993, p. 21).

Just as significant was the absence in the design of a system that would be able to handle the occurrence of problems. Indeed, Robin Bloomfield, a consultant who has advised the UK government on the of safety of computer-controlled systems, commented:

With about a million calls a year the system has to be more reliable than a nuclear protection system. I would expect to see a detailed safety case for justifying its operation, and several different backup systems (*The Independent* 30 October 1992).

The new system was to have a big impact on the work of both the call takers and allocators at Central Ambulance Control and ambulance staff themselves. The move to Phase III of the proposed system was perhaps the most fundamental change since it was intended to automate the decision-making process and:

substitute a set of rules within a computer program for the judgement and understanding of controllers, usually with excess of 15 years experience of London's ambulances, a local knowledge of traffic flow, the position of hospitals, short cuts and medical knowledge (NUPE, Submission, 1992, p. 39).

Perhaps at the heart of all these factors was the dream to use a single leading-edge technological fix to improve poor performance and automate out staff problems. The system design, with its dramatic implications for existing staff practice, demonstrates a belief that the creation of CAD could change local working practices by simply designing them out of the system. Such wishful thinking indicates a naive approach to the use of technology.

The new system was to be introduced into a context in which there had been recent restructuring, staff redundancies and reallocation, low morale, lack of confidence in management, and very poor labour relations. These factors, in themselves, hardly presented the best situation in which to select what was recognized as a high-risk strategy as the solution to the problems of the LAS. But these were not the only factors.

The same team who did most of the work on the systems requirement specification were also responsible for the technical evaluation of the tenders for the contract to build the new system. The people with the most responsibility for creating the System Requirement Specification (SRS) for a leading-edge system would seem to have been an outside contractor and a non-technical manager.

That the system was unable to move controllably in the event of a system crash to operating on the backup server was due not only to the failure to test the fallback procedures but also to changes made in the system design. The addition of printers to the original design was intended to enable a partial system to be up and running on the original implementation date of 8 January 1992. It was the effects of this change, originally a short-term fix, that caused the fallback procedures to fail (Page *et al.*, 1993, p. 56).

Management ethos

Perhaps the most important group of factors that enabled events to take the path they did were the many changes that the LAS underwent and the corporate culture that developed as a result. The creation of the LAS as a separate entity and the appointment of a tough new Chief Executive to improve its performance were key events that led to massive reorganization and a reduction of around 20% in the number of managers. It was never going to be easy to improve the performance of the LAS, and John Wilby, then Chief Executive, believed it to be a 'five-year job', but recognized that the biggest challenge was in 'effecting cultural change' (quoted in *Health Service Journal* 4 June 1992, p. 11). However, it was alleged during the offical inquiry that the culture created was one of 'fear of failure' in which the pressure to succeed outweighed virtually any other consideration. Indeed, the Inquiry report commented that the existence of such a culture

> ... may have put undue pressure on management directly
> concerned with CAD to ensure that the system was implemented
> to timetable and to budget. This may have blinded them to some
> of the fundamental difficulties with the system that perhaps in
> retrospect seem rather more obvious.

Similar views on management style and corporate culture within the LAS were provided by a former Press Officer:

> Having worked for the Service until last year I know how damaging the recently deposed regime's arrogant and confrontational style was to an organization whose strengths have always been the calibre and character of its staff.... They [the new management] quickly alienated ambulance officers. With morale already at rock bottom and standards of service unacceptably low, it seems amazing that the situation is arguably worse now than during the [previous industrial] dispute itself. All the worst aspects of the market approach have contributed to the decline: an expensive concentration on corporate image; the employing of an army of management consultants; the deliberate failure to consult staff over major changes; and the spending of vast sums of scarce resources on glossy projects at the expense of basic patient care (NUPE Submission 1992, p. 7, quoting a letter by Mark Sudbury in *The Guardian* 3 November 1992).

The setting of the original £1.5 million budget and 8 January 1992 deadline can both be traced back to decisions that were accepted by the Board of the LAS. Given the importance of the decisions the Board would make, an informed discussion is essential, yet it was claimed by Dennis Boyd, CBE, a member of the Inquiry Team and former Chief Conciliation Officer of ACAS (Advisory Conciliation and Arbitration Service), that

> They appointed people to the Board who were probably not sure of their responsibility. Some of their decisions were clearly rubber-stamping (*Health Service Journal*, 4 March 1993).

A lack of effective control at the top combined with an inability to manage lower down and a fear-based culture is not likely to produce an atmosphere in which doubts can be mentioned and problems discussed. But it seems it was in this kind of context in which a largely untested system with a history of problems went live with *two* problems classified as 'serious service degradation' still outstanding.

Procurement process

The restrictions on implementation date and the outline cost of the new system were sufficient to skew the whole procurement process. Given the final selection of a proposal that included a small and (in the provision of safety-critical command and control systems) inexperienced software house, it is significant that the evaluation checklist did not specifically attach any weight to supplier experience in this area. It later emerged (Page *et al*, 1993, pp. 25–7) that Systems Options had no experience in designing or acquiring mission-critical systems for emergency services and, given their low quote for developing the CAD software, may have underestimated what was involved. This is easy to say with hindisght.

The procurement guidelines that were used to award the contract were also deeply flawed. The deadline for final implementation, 8 January 1992, was set by the Chief Executive of the LAS without discussion with the LAS Board. The outline budget of around £1.5 million seems to have been similarly arbitrary, but could have had its origins in a misunderstanding of the Arthur Andersen report commissioned in late 1990 to examine the previous failing systems project, and recommend future directions. The report stated that if a packaged solution were available a budget of £1.5 million may be appropriate, with an overall development time of 19 months. However, it goes on to indicate that if a packaged solution was not available these estimates should be significantly increased. It seems that the Director of Support Services, who was directly responsible for the new system, was never shown the Andersen report.

It will be recalled that the checklist against which each of the proposals were evaluated included such factors as 'ability to perform the task required', 'ability to handle throughput and response times', 'ability to meet timetable' and 'cost'. However, within the selection process that actually took place, the inability of a proposal to meet virtually the complete functional requirement or the deadline led to its rejection. In fact, proposals that could not meet the timetable did not make the shortlist. It seems that the ability of a supplier to meet what was later admitted to be an absurdly short deadline was accorded far greater importance than was originally indicated.

Timetable

That the timetable under which the system was to be developed was totally unrealistic was recognized by many within the LAS and its suppliers to be so. A representative of Systems Options stated that in our contract signed in July 1991, it was stipulated that the system would be introduced in its entirety in January 1992. I don't believe that was realistic (quoted in NUPE Submission, 1992, p. 40).

Paul Williams, one of the Inquiry Team, commented that 'The timetable was impossible, and we use that term advisedly' (The Guardian, 26 February 1993).

Contributory Causes

Inexperience of supplier

The Inquiry Report states (p. 27) that Systems Options was a well-established small software house that had gained a good reputation for their work. However, in taking responsibility for the LAS development it was suggested that they were attempting to deal with a project that was far larger than anything they had handled previously. If this is the case it is highly probable that, as the development proceeded, they quickly got out of their depth.

The Inquiry Team stated that, given the very tight deadline that was imposed and the complexity of the system, no software house could have delivered a workable solution. The major difference, however, is that a more experienced software house might be expected to have recognized the danger signs early enough to have taken some sort of action—though that may be wishful thinking.

Inadequate testing

A further weakness in the development process was the inadequate level of testing that appears to have taken place. Functional testing, the testing of individual parts of a system to see if they operate according to specification, should be only a first step in ensuring that a system will work as expected. The Inquiry Report revealed (pp. 31–5) that at no stage before final implementation was the entire CAD system tested in anything like the kind of live conditions under which it would have to operate. No tests had been devised or carried out to examine the behaviour of the system if the data it received were incorrect or incomplete, nor was any attempt made to test the communications systems upon which the whole structure was utterly dependent. Even the procedures surrounding an orderly fallback to backup operation if problems with the primary server arose were untested. 26 October 1992—the day the system went live across the whole of London—was in effect the first time a full-scale test of the whole system had been attempted.

The combination of the Windows environment and the use of a newly released Visual Basic development tool was also never tested. See below (Graceful Degradation) for more detail.

Poor Quality Assurance (QA)

In the high-pressure situation of chasing unrealistic deadlines software Quality Assurance seems to have been minimal. The Inquiry Report suggests that Systems Options often worked outside the official Project Issue Report (PIR) system of formalizing the notification and correction of identified problems, with Systems Options staff making untested on-the-spot changes to software. Such a practice would have meant that not only was it very difficult to keep track of system changes but it would also reduce the effect of the PIR system and also undermine the testing regime, as undocumented changes were made to previously tested software.

No independent checks or controls of QA procedures seem to have been in place. Early in the development the project team had received a QA proposal from a company associated with one of the unsuccessful tenders to build the new system. The company, ISL Consultancy Services, prepared a submission to which they received no reply:

> We were never able after submission to talk...in spite of repeated attempts. This was an extreme discourtesy possibly due to our determined approach to the proposal to produce a true QA and not a rubber stamp to the project team (NUPE Submission, 1992, p. 44).

It subsequently transpired that the root cause of the LAS system crash on 4 November 1992 was poor software QA. Around three weeks before the system locked up some program code had been left in the system by a programmer engaged on development work. The effect of this piece of leftover code was that every time a vehicle was mobilized the system would allocate and not release a small amount of memory within the server. This meant that over the three weeks since it was inserted into the system the bug had reserved virtually all available memory, eventually causing the system to crash due to insufficient memory.

Poor training

The training of Central Ambulance Control staff was based around staff competence to perform specific jobs. Once a competence had been obtained it was 'signed off' by both the trainer and the trainee. However doubts were expressed about the overall quality of the training. Providing a consistent level of training was made very difficult by the fact that the system itself was constantly changing as modifications were made.

There was a considerable delay between the date most staff were trained and when the system was eventually implemented. This meant that there was a gap between staff being trained and actually using the system, with the effect that the effectiveness of the training would have been reduced. Indeed, staff representatives later commented:

> At the end of January 1992 the first . . . stages of the CAD system became live without any meaningful consultation on training, staffing, health and safety, ergonomics, duties and responsibilities with representatives of the staff who have to operate it in the control room or respond to it on the road. Control staff were given just two days' general training to familiarize themselves with this new system. . . . Staff naturally concluded that their skills and experience were no longer valued. In the future the CAD system was merely to require keyboarding skills, with all life and death decisions to be taken by computer (NUPE Submission, 1992, p. 38).

The problem was perhaps exacerbated by the decision to train ambulance and central control room staff separately. This decision, combined with an already strained management–staff relationship and the imposition of an anonymous automated despatching system in which voice contact between ambulances and control room was largely eliminated, is not one likely to encourage a partnership between control room and ambulance staff in making the best of the new system.

Inadequate project management

Management of the process of turning the design into reality was confused with responsibility for project management being passed from

Apricot to Systems Options, eventually coming to rest with the LAS itself. The project was managed by the Director of Support Services and the contract analyst—in addition to their other workloads.

The instruction to use the PRINCE project management methodology (a government requirement) presumably gave some comfort to senior managers. The reality was, however, that not only did the LAS Project Team itself (including the Director of Support Services and the contract analyst) have virtually no previous project management experience of any kind, but also neither they nor Systems Options had any experience of PRINCE. Given such a lack of experience the instruction to use the PRINCE project management methodology was largely futile, despite the introductory course on the use of PRINCE run for members of the project team. As a result, little meaningful use was made of PRINCE during the project.

Given the unrealistic completion date, even if an experienced project manager had taken charge, it would still have been very unlikely that the system could have been completed on time. However, many of the problems that delayed its completion would probably have been identified far sooner, and delays minimized.

Lessons of the LAS Experience

Organizational Lessons

The establishment in 1990 of a new management structure was perceived by some to be a key event in the development of the computerized ambulance despatch project. The tough management style adopted by the new regime coupled with a perceived refusal to engage in meaningful consultation with staff added a new dimension to what was a deeply demoralized organization—fear of failure (Page *et al.*, 1993, p. 40).

So what is the lesson here—that managers dissent and get sacked? No, the lesson is that fear-based cultures can create a climate in which bad decisions and poor work can, with ill luck, grow to become major disasters simply through fearful silence within the management structure. This case amply demonstrates this fact.

The factor that acted to reinforce this was the perceived lack of trust by management and the subsequent marginalization of LAS staff representatives. In such a culture it might be felt that requests to reconsider decisions, or to highlight fundamental operational problems with the new system, would be viewed as Luddite and discounted. Thus a break with reality is created.

On paper the LAS had an organizational structure that showed a direct line of responsibility and accountability that went from the CEO and Executive Directors, to the Board, and ultimately to the Regional Health Authority. The Board would examine all major decisions and monitor the progress of major developments like the computerization project. However, this also does not take into account the weakness of the structure if the Board is content, as was claimed, to rubber-stamp CEO decisions and does not wish to become proactive in their steward-ship role. If the body or organization ultimately responsible, in this case the RHA, fails to exercise its right to examine progress (even when problems appear to exist), then the structure is pretty worthless. Organi-zational structures have to be made to work by the individuals within them.

The problem of poor oversight was recognized in the recommenda-tions of the Inquiry Report that:

> The precise role, function and responsibilities of the Chair and non-Executive Directors of the LAS Board are agreed in writing
> between those members of the Board and the South West Thames RHA. It is important that all non-Executive Directors have the
> time, commitment and experience to undertake the functions required;
> The Chief Executive should remain accountable to the LAS Board, and its Chair, and through them to the RGM (Regional General
> Management). The issues on which Board discussion and approval are required should be clarified as should the topics on which the
> Board should receive regular reports;
> Executive Directors should remain accountable to the Board, and personally accountable to the Chief Executive;
> Personal objectives of the Chief Executive, Executive Directors and senior managers should derive from corporate objectives agreed
> between the LAS Board and South West Thames RHA. Regular reviews would thus be undertaken as part of the two-way

corporate review and Individual Performance Review (IPR)
programme and difficulties in meeting agreed targets and objectives
identified at an early stage...'

The reorganization of the LAS in 1991, with the loss of 20% of
managers, resulted in the span of control for managers and Directors
alike being too great. The Director of Support Services, in addition to
fulfilling his other responsibilities, was also acting (by default) as a
project manager for the ambulance despatch development. The CEO
was driving this development, and everything else. This left no-one to
stand back and look at the 'big picture' of what was actually going on.
The creation of an IS Steering Group, in addition to the project
committee, charged with the role of overseeing developments would
have provided the opportunity to take a rather more impartial view
than was possible. The old adage about swamps and crocodiles is
perfectly illustrated by the LAS failure. Unless there is a clear distinction
between those staff actively engaged in a project and the people who are
supposed to oversee its progress, the 'big picture' will inevitably be lost
from view.

The Inquiry Report recommended:

> The establishment of a Project Subcommittee of the LAS Board.
> That LAS recruit an IT Director, who will have direct access to the
> LAS Board.
> That consideration is given urgently to a further restructuring of
> management.
> i   To lessen the span of control of some Executive Directors;
> ii To implement an experienced and effective level of
>   management, with delegated responsibility and authority for
>   decision-making, to deal with day-to-day operational issues on
>   a divisional basis within London.

Human Factors

Over-commitment

One factor that over-committed behaviour has in common with the
fear-based culture discussed above is the failure to keep in touch with
reality. Taken to extremes, as it seems to have been within some parts

of the LAS, the desire to attain the goal will displace good judgement and even common sense. The focus on a narrow goal can result in individuals or groups becoming victims of 'groupthink' and ignoring a wide range of outside factors. The term 'groupthink' was introduced by Irving L. Janis to define the situation in which groups of individuals can become so focused upon a course of action that realistic appraisals of alternatives are excluded. As we have seen, this behaviour can lead to disastrous results unless staff are required to involve those outside the group. The role of an impartial IS Steering Committee or other group of external reviewers can be important in this respect.

Consultation

An important part of any new system introduction is that the various groups who will have to use it, the stakeholders, have been involved in its development from an early stage. The LAS failed badly in this respect. The apparent policy to marginalize staff representatives meant that the ambulance staff—a vital user group—were not consulted in the early stages of system's development. Given the fact that the system depended utterly upon ambulance staff it was a total folly to exclude them. Rather they should have been part of a wider consultative process that would have allowed key staff groups to make their own contribution to the final shape of the system and thus 'buy-in' to the changes that will result.

The same lesson applies to any IS development. The history of IS usage in organizations is littered with examples of systems that were either never used or were under-used because of poor consultation. This danger is recognized within the Inquiry Report which states that any future system '...must have total ownership by management and staff, both within the CAC [Central Ambulance Control] and the ambulance crews.

Design Lessons

The design of the computerized despatch system was, as we have seen, flawed. However, while technology could provide the solution to the problems of ambulance despatch, the manner in which it was applied was naive and unrealistic. In the words of Ian Lund (at that time the managing partner of ISL Consultancy), 'The use of computer-based systems in command and control is correct ... but it cannot be achieved (a) on the cheap, and (b) without proven experts' (quoted in NUPE Submission, 1992, p. 34). This comment can be applied to the development of any computer-based information system.

Beware of the Technological Fix

One major problem with the design of the LAS system was that it may have carried with it a hidden agenda. On this agenda was the eradication of a number of working practices that would, in the eyes of management, improve the efficiency of the service.

It was always very unlikely that the attempt to remove these practices through the use of technology, rather than by negotiation and consultation, would work. The staff whose working practices need to change must be involved in the process of effecting that change. There is no short-cut solution. Technology doesn't solve industrial relations problems—managers do. There is no such thing as an easy technological fix.

Graceful Degradation

How does a system react when things start to go wrong? The major problem with the LAS system was (it appears) that the concept of a measured approach to problems did not occur to the designers. The system slowed down under load in any case. What happened when problems began to pile up was that it collapsed under the load of its own error messages.

The decision to select a user-friendly Windows interface and to use Visual Basic (Visual Basic is a programming tool to enable fast systems development—unfortunately, Visual Basic applications were relatively slow when running) were, in themselves, key factors in the overall level of performance that the system could provide. The result was an interface that was so slow in operation that users attempted to speed up the system by opening every application they would need at the start of their shift (each in a separate window), and then using the Windows multi-tasking environment to move between them as required. This highly memory-intensive method of working would have had the effect of reducing system performance still further.

Mission-critical (or safety-critical) systems need to be designed to cope with problems in an orderly fashion. The concept of 'Graceful Degradation', in this context, means that the system should not just fall over, but should continue to operate at a reduced level, hopefully long enough to enable problems to be rectified. This may be achieved by software design or by backup systems, but contingency should be built into the overall system.

Procurement Lessons

This case is a prime example of how not to procure an information system. Not only did key staff in the procurement process lack the experience to specify a computerized despatch system, they seem to have taken a rigid approach to the process of selection.

The validation process was similarly flawed, with the external assessor and the LAS Board adopting the 'lowest-bidder' approach to supplier selection. It is likely that the low budget and tight deadline also played their parts in this process, but the organization and the people within it failed to recognize that it was dealing with something it did not understand.

If the proposal to accept a tender is subject to external review, as it should be with large system, then it must be truly impartial and the terms of reference must extend to include not just the probity of the process, but also the technical merit of the bid. (The external audit of the probity of the tender process was undertaken by the Systems Manager of another ambulance service). In addition, supplier experience, resources and thus competence (as well as supplier references) should be investigated in some detail before a bid is accepted.

The weakness of the procurement process was recognized in the following recommendation:

> that the standing financial instructions should be extended to provide more qualitative guidance for future major IT procurements.

In the wake of this IS disaster (and a number of others) the NHS issued a detailed set of guidelines governing the procurement of computer systems. POISE (Procurement of Information Systems Effectively), consists of guidelines on best practice and a set of standard procurement stages and tools, and is now widely used throughout the NHS.

Postscript

On 28 October 1992, two days after the implementation and amid intense criticism, the Chief Executive of the LAS resigned[4] and the Health Secretary announced an enquiry into the events that had led up to the abortive implementation. Once the Inquiry report was published, in February 1993, the Chairman of the LAS also resigned (Watts, 1993; Bicknell, 1993; Hayward, 1993).

Since the resignations took place the LAS has once again been reorganized, although this time in line with the detailed recommendations of the Inquiry Report. The scale of operations within London have been reflected by the modification to divisional structure to create a Central Division, with much of the decision making for each Division now being devolved to newly created Divisional Directors. The need for more attention to be paid to professional development across the entire LAS was recognized by splitting the responsibilities of the old Director of Human Resources on the LAS Board between the new roles of Personnel Director and Director of Organizational Development. Finally, in recognition of the importance technology will play in the future development of the LAS, an IT Director was appointed to the Board.

When the CAD system finally crashed in late 1992 the LAS reverted to the use of the tried and tested manual system of resource allocation. The LAS has continued to use parts of the manual system, preferring to take a very cautious approach to the use of IT in a safety-critical application. The hard lessons of the disaster appear to have been well learnt by an LAS determined not to repeat the mistakes of the past by rushing to implement yet another computer aided despatch system. The Inquiry Report recommended that the next attempt should be on something like a four-year time scale, with a budget of around £4 million.

——————........

[4] This was widely reported at the time in a range of publications, including Hayward (1992) and Smith *et al.* (1992).

VARIATIONS ON A THEME

The potential benefits from taking a leap in technology is, as we have seen, often pretty risky yet apparently hard to resist. The case of the Denver baggage handling system illustrates how easy it is to fall into the technology trap.

The Denver Baggage Disaster[5]

Delays at airports are nothing new, but the problems surrounding the opening of the new Denver International Airport (DIA) produced delays of months and millions of dollars of additional costs. The cause of the problem: an advanced baggage-handling system that refused to work.

The scale of the DIA made it one of the largest public works projects of its time, with the airport covering 13 726 hectares—roughly twice the size of Manhattan. The sophisticated baggage-handling system was designed to automate away many of the manual operations associated with older systems and provide a fast and efficient means of moving passenger baggage around the airport. The system, originally costing around $193 million (£129 million), was designed to be able to move up to 1700 bags per minute from the check-in desks in the main terminal to any of the many unloading stations in one of the three separate concourses. It would also be able to move arriving passenger baggage and deposit it at the correct carousel and, perhaps most importantly for the DIA to be an efficient hub airport, automatically transfer baggage between connecting flights.

The highly automated baggage system that was to achieve this seamless integration was to use more than 4000 telecars running over 20 miles of track that is linked to some six miles of conveyer belt. Each telecar would generally carry a single piece of luggage, with special double-length telecars being used for skis or irregular-shaped loads. The entire baggage operation was designed to be automatic with traffic being automatically switched by a combination of the 100 computers,

---

[5] The details in this case are sourced from *IEEE Spectrum* (1994), *Rocky Mountain News* (1994) and *Computerworld* (1994).

56 laser scanners and telecar-based radio transponders employed within the system. The destination for any piece of baggage would either be entered manually at the check-in or be read by the laser scanners from barcoded tags attached to the luggage. Photo–electric cells located around the track were intended to monitor telecar traffic and prevent traffic jams occurring.

While the design was impressive on paper it was less so in practice, with tests resulting in telecars either piling up or jamming the tracks, bags falling off or being damaged, and luggage taking too long or being sent to the wrong destination. The problems were so severe, and the airport so dependent upon its baggage-handling system, that the opening of the airport was moved first from October 1993 to March 1994, then to May 1994, and again to the end of February 1995. The cost of these delays were running at around a $1 million (£600 000) a day, with some $500 000 (£300 000) of this amount relating to the interest costs on the $3.2 billion bond issue raised by the city of Denver.

The causes of this problem? Reports centred on the two factors of time and complexity. On time it was reported that the time allowed to build and test what was a highly advanced leading-edge system, some two years, was half what was actually required. On complexity Professor Richard deNeufville of MIT was quoted as saying that:

> The enormous increase in complexity that distinguishes the automated system at Denver from all others looks much more than a single-generation evolution of technology. . . . It is more like an attempted leap from the third to the fifth of sixth generation of baggage systems.

Indeed, he goes further to state that:

> It is not clear that anyone, anywhere, is currently capable of managing the automated baggage system at DIA to ensure on-time performance, or is likely to be able to, at any time in the near future.

While the system has been simplified and its reliability improved dramatically, no-one was taking any chances for the February 1995 deadline. In August 1994 a separate manual baggage-handling system based on traditional tugs and carts was ordered to be built to act as a backup to the automated system, at a cost of some \$63 million (£42 million). The system finally went live in February 1995.

References

Bicknell, D., 'Any takers for a stretcher case?' *Computing Weekly*, 4 March 14 (1993).

Computerworld, 'United to simplify Denver's troubled baggage project', 10 October (1994).

Hayward D., 'LAS bosses ignored warnings', *Computing*, 5 November, 1 (1992).

Hayward, D., 'LAS chiefs slammed over systems disaster', *Computing*, 4 March, 6 (1993).

IEEE Spectrum, 'Baggage-handling snags hold new airport at the gate', August (1994).

Mullin, J., 'Management failures spanned several years', *The Independent*, 26 February, 3 (1993).

National Audit Office, *National Health Service: Patient Transport Services*, July (1990).

NUPE, *999—The London Misery Line*, September, (1992).

Page, D., Williams, P. and Boyd, D., *Report of the Inquiry into the London Ambulance Service*, South West Thames Regional Health Authority, February (1993).

Rocky Mountain News, 'Original luggage system was too high tech to work', 26 December (1994).

Smith, M. *et al.*, 'Flood of calls caused 999 chaos', *Daily Telegraph*, 29 October, 2 (1992).

Watts, S., 'Report prompts resignation of ambulance boss', *The Independent*, 26 February, 1 (1993).

5

THE LONDON STOCK EXCHANGE *TAURUS*

. . . .

Building the invisible palace[1]

[1] Sir Andrew Hugh Smith, Chairman of the London Stock Exchange, describing the Taurus system. Quoted in *Financial Times*, 12 March 1993, p. 11.

Chronology of Major Events

1979	Talisman system implemented
1987	Taurus system is proposed based on a single central database to maintain all share records. Predicted cost of £60 million
Sept. 1988	Review of Taurus undertaken. Design abandoned due to projected cost and widespread opposition from Share Registrars.
1989	Siscot (Securities Industries Steering Committee on Taurus) formed. Proposes new version of Taurus
Aug. 1989	Exchange brings in a Coopers & Lybrand partner as project director. Delay announced on first phase of Taurus, originally due in October 1989
Jan. 1990	SE targets October 1991 for launch of Taurus
Feb. 1990	London Stock Exchange expects final bill for Taurus to be £40–£50 million
March 1990	Taurus project offically launched Target date set for Taurus of October 1991
May 1990	Exchange predicts Taurus will save City of London £250 million over next 10 years
Sept. 1990	US-designed VSPS securities processing package purchased at a cost of £2.2 million due to insufficient time to develop own system Target date for Taurus October 1991
May 1991	After long delay Department of Trade and Industry publishes new legal framework Target date for Taurus moved to May 1992
Dec. 1991	Formal regulations providing the legal framework for Taurus finally laid before parliament after more than a year's delay
Jan. 1992	Anderson Consulting called in to run a three month Technology Transformation Programme to overhaul IT operation. Review is not to include Taurus
Feb. 1992	New legal framework for Taurus becomes law, enabling final specifications to be completed
April 1992	Anderson Consulting contracted to rationalize then run IT operations. Taurus is excluded from the deal.
Sept. 1992	Anderson Consulting, who were to run Taurus once complete, undertake an examination of Taurus
Dec. 1992	Report from Anderson Consulting suggests serious problems with Taurus

Jan. 1993   Introduction of Taurus postponed until Spring 1994. Wider testing commences. External consultant brought in to run technical side of project. Full review of Taurus ordered

Feb. 1993   As result of review it is predicted that Taurus would take another three years to build and that costs would double

March 1993   Taurus project cancelled at a cost to the Stock Exchange of £75 million and the loss of 350 jobs.
               Bank of England announces task force to look into share settlement arrangements on the London stock market

July 1993   Bank of England produces design brief for its paperless share settlement system, to be called Crest, and announces intention to develop detailed specifications over a six- to nine-month period

July 1996   Crest goes live. The Crest system, made simpler than Taurus, was developed over three years and at a cost of £29 million.

The failure of the Taurus development rocked the City of London and the Stock Exchange to its roots. One of the most high-profile IS projects in the UK and the largest development in Europe was to have revolutionized share trading yet foundered at a cost of hundreds of millions of pounds. The case looks at the background and progress of the development and examines how the initial conception was later to be fatally flawed by compromise and poor management. The causes of the failure are analysed and important lessons on the management of systems development projects are drawn.

Introduction

If any one type of organization can be said to represent the information age it must surely be the stock exchanges of the world. The vision of share traders sitting in front of computer terminals making deals worth millions at the touch of a button is a potent image. This is the information economy in action with billions of shares being traded daily across the world in the big financial centres of New York, Tokyo, and London.

But behind the frantic scenes of the dealing rooms complex systems must exist to record share ownership and deal with the share transfers and the payment that concludes a deal. Given the amount of trading that takes place each day, this is a mammoth task that will only get larger with the development of the world economy and global trading.

For a stock exchange that is fully automated the prospect of a continual growth in the volume of transactions is only to be welcomed. However, for an exchange that still relies upon the mass transfer of paper share certificates this prospect represents a real problem. The London Stock Exchange was just such an organization, and this is the story of how they tried and ultimately failed to introduce Taurus, their paperless share trading system.

The 'Big Bang' took place in October 1986 and represented a fundamental change in the way stocks and shares were traded on the Stock Exchange. Prior to the Big Bang all share trading was a paper-based process that demanded the movement of large volumes of paper around the City. The Big Bang marked the first stage in what later came to be called the 'dematerialization' of share certificates and the adoption of paperless trading.

On the Stock Exchange share prices are set by a number of large stockbroking firms called 'Market Makers', who account for a large percentage of overall share trading. Only these Market Makers who were to be involved in this first move towards paperless trading. In order to avoid giving any one of these firms an unfair advantage over the others it was decided that they should all move to paperless share trading at the same time. Such a method of moving between old and new systems is often referred to by computing professionals as the 'Big Bang' approach. Once the mass media had picked it up the term 'Big Bang' was to be forever linked to the movement to paperless trading between Market Makers on the Stock Exchange.

The *London Stock Exchange* (SE) was established in 1773 as a market in which companies could raise capital by selling shares in their venture. Shareholders, the name given to individuals who own shares, were also able to use the SE to buy and sell their shareholdings.

Stockbrokers, or Brokers, buy and sell shares in Public Companies on behalf of shareholders who who do not have direct access to the SE.

Public Companies (also known as Listed Companies) are so called because their shares may be bought and sold on the SE at prices set by the Market Makers.

Market Makers are large stockbroking firms who set the price of every share that is traded on the SE. There are 32 Market Makers and since 1986 they have been able to trade between themselves electronically.

Share *Registrars* maintain detailed registers of the names and rights of individual shareholders for Listed Companies. Every time a share in a Listed Company is bought or sold the share register for that company must be updated by the Registrar. A very high percentage of the share registry business on the SE is dominated by three large commercial banks.

The Taurus Development

With a history that stretches back to the late 1960s, the move to paperless share transfers at the SE has been a long time coming. The introduction in 1979 of Talisman, a system for settling share deals that was entirely computer based, represented a first step down the road to entirely paperless trading. The success of the Talisman system led to the proposal in 1981 to extend automation to the market as a whole and to end the use of paper share certificates. Work on the system, later to be called Taurus (Transfer and Automated Registration of Uncertificated Stock), commenced in 1983.

The year 1986 was a landmark is the history of the London Stock Exchange since it marked the introduction of electronic dealing for UK shares. The most obvious effect of the 'Big Bang' apart from the introduction of electronic share dealing was that the trading floor of the Stock Exchange building was abandoned by the big stockbroking firms in favour of the remote computer terminal. But the Big Bang was only a partial transformation since it left in place many of the existing methods of working, including the requirement to record ownership using paper share certificates.

It is a requirement under UK law that all publicly traded companies keep a register of their shareholders. While some very large organizations, such as British Gas, maintain their own list, the majority employ a professional registrar. It is thus the registrar's job to deal with the trail of paper that is generated from the process of buying and selling shares. And a lot of paper there was, since the very simplest share trade on the SE involved at least three pieces of paper being shuffled between six places. In fact, the privatization's of the mid-1980s created a crisis as the City of London began to drown under the welter of paper created as a result of a rapid rise in share trading. At its peak in August 1987 a backlog of nearly 650 000 deals with a value of £8 billion ($12 billion) was built up, so large was the volume of shares being traded. The cost of financing these unsettled bargains, together with the expense of hiring the hundreds of extra staff needed to clear the logjam, was estimated to be as large as £50 million ($75 million). Due to the rising market, the risks being run at that time mainly fell on the buyers of stock, who could not be sure that the sellers would actually deliver on their deal and thus faced the risk of having to replace a failed purchase at a higher price. This situation was dramatically reversed with the market crash of 19 October, with the sellers of stock facing the prospect that buyers would renege on deals. The intention of the Taurus project to replace paper share certificates with an entry, like a bank balance, on an electronic register would have solved many of the problems that the stock market faced at that time by reducing the time lag between deal and payment.

The version of the Taurus project that had been under development since 1983 proposed that information on shares and shareholders would be located in a single large database that would be administered by the SE. Under this proposal the procedures surrounding the buying and selling of shares would be streamlined and changes in ownership would be achieved simply by account transfer. A major problem with the proposal, from the professional share registrars' point of view, was that their business could disappear overnight as share registrations were transferred to the huge new database to be run by the SE. As a result of this and other problems the original Taurus proposal met with strong opposition from a number of sources who wished to maintain the inefficient, but highly profitable, status quo.

Despite this opposition, the SE continued to work on the project until late 1988 when, after independent reviews, it was concluded that the project in its current form should be scrapped. In addition to the opposition from vested interests, the projected £60 million ($90 million) cost was considered to be too high and the technical complexity too great. Studies at the time apparently showed that it would require the entire resources of two IBM 3090 mainframes and that to handle the daily transactions in the trillion or more shares in issue on the SE data would have to be spread over 560 disk drives, each loaded to only 3% of its capacity in order to provide the necessary response times.

After the demise of what came to be termed Taurus 1 the Bank of England became involved and was instrumental in the creation of an industry-wide committee. The main task of this committee, called Siscot (Securities and Investment Steering Committee on Taurus), was to design a paperless settlement process that was acceptable to banks, securities houses, investors and registrars.

By spring 1989 the Siscot committee recommended that the best way forward was to expand the existing settlement system, Talisman, used by the Market Makers on the SE. Under the Talisman system the Market Makers trade and settle deals between themselves through a series of nominee accounts in a system called Sepon (Stock Exchange Pool Nominee). Under this system paperless share transfers are carried out simply by moving entries between computer-based accounts. This process, also called book-entry transfer, enables ownership of shares to be transferred without issuing new share certificates and forms the basis of a paperless trading system. The Sepon proposal envisaged extending these paperless facilities from the 32 Market Makers to include around 1000 institutional investors, banks, stockbrokers and other financial intermediaries that would hold the shares on behalf of individuals in sub-registers. The advantages of this proposal were that, at around £10 million, it was relatively cheap, and that it could be phased in slowly with minimum disruption to the operation of the market as a whole.

The basis of the Sepon design was that all shares were to be held on behalf of clients in accounts controlled by organizations like brokers and registrars. Under this design these organizations, known as Taurus Account Controllers or TACs, would be responsible for maintaining the sole record of their clients' shareholdings. This not only undermined the role of registrars and increased the costs of stockbrokers but also made it much harder for listed companies to find out who their shareholders were. The changes that were adopted meant that TACs would be able to opt out of the responsibility to maintain records of client shareholdings, passing on the task to the specialist registrars. The effect of this change was to preserve within Taurus the existing paper-based way of operating (only without the paper) in parallel with the new system based around TACs. This design meant that stockbrokers were now in a position to avoid the technology and other costs of becoming a Taurus Account Controller and registrars were able to continue to maintain the share registers of listed companies. However, it also continued to provide for the parallel situation where the sole records of shareholdings were maintained by institutional investors, banks and those stockbrokers who wished to do so.

This proposal did, however, raise objections from large UK organizations on the grounds that they would no longer be able to track easily the precise ownership of their shares. This was a side-effect of extending the system of nominee accounts so that the only name that could officially appear on the registers of publicly quoted companies would be that of the institutional investor, bank or stockbroker who bought the shares for their client. Updates of the register of shareholders would be provided on request, with any transfers within the sub-registers of large movements of shares being notified immediately in order to guard against hostile take-over bids. But the fear remained that, in a hostile market, any loss of visibility was to be discouraged.

A further objection to the Sepon proposal was that it assumed that the new system would run alongside, rather than replace, the existing paper-based system. This would mean that there would be two parallel systems for registering shares, through share certificates and electronically, and would impose an added transitional cost to moving to the new system. The question also arose as to when, if ever, it would be possible to eliminate share certificates.

The opposition to Sepon grew, and alternative proposals were made that would make it easier for company executives to see updated lists of their shareholders by allowing registrars to maintain most of their traditional functions. One proposal would require company registrars to keep parallel updated registers of shareholders, incorporating all the data held in the sub-registers, thereby ensuring visibility of ownership.

In August 1989 a consultant on secondment from Deloitte Haskins & Sells (later to become part of Coopers & Lybrand) was appointed as Director of the Taurus project which had until this time been run by the SE itself. This same person, a previous deputy chief executive of the SE, had acted as the project director during development of the Talisman system between 1975 and 1979. His appointment was made in order to strengthen the management team as the project entered the next phase of its development. One of the first tasks that the newly installed Director had to perform was to announce that project Taurus would be delayed by three months, pushing its implementation date to late 1990.

By Autumn 1989 the opposition to the Taurus design then being proposed had grown. The dissenters to the Sepon approach, primarily stockbrokers and listed companies, had voiced strong doubts about the viability of the chosen system, ensuring Siscot undertake a full review of their alternative design. As a result, extensive changes were made to the Sepon design that would benefit the three most vocal opposition groups: stockbrokers, listed companies and registrars.

It was this design, which embodied in a single system both old and new ways of working, that formed the basis for the Taurus system that was to be built.

In March 1990 Taurus was launched and a detailed document entitled *Project Taurus: A Prospectus for Settlement in the 1990s* was published. While this was in no way a technical specification for Taurus it provided a detailed analysis of how the proposed system would work for the stockbrokers, banks and other financial institutions that were to use it.

The architecture of the proposed system was radically different from the original design for Taurus. While the original version was based on a single central database, the final version was to be a distributed database with the SE acting as a central hub.

The project timetable (see Figure 5.1) published in the prospectus indicated that basic design work on Taurus would be completed by September 1990, with detailed user documentation being issued shortly afterwards. The switch from moving data using paper and magnetic tape to using computer communications would commence in March 1991, with large institutions moving to full paperless trading in October of that year. The move to paperless trading, or 'dematerialization' as it was termed at the time, was scheduled to be completed by the end of 1993.

The cost–benefit analysis contained in the prospectus, based on work done by Coopers & Lybrand, concluded that the elimination of paper handling would result in substantial cost reductions. Assuming the elimination of paper share certificates, it was predicted that direct cost savings over ten years could amount to £255 million ($382 million), with addi-

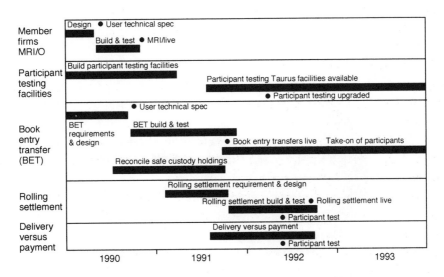

Figure 5.1 Settlement implementation timetable

tional savings coming from the reduction in both the risks and the capital associated with share trading. Predicted intangible benefits included the simplification of trading processes and the increased confidence in the UK market by overseas investors.

The development cost of the project from April 1989 to March 1993 were estimated to be between £45 million and £50 million ($68–75 million), with this amount being split between infrastructure, dematerialization and settlement costs. This is illustrated in Figure 5.2. It was predicted that approximately 40% of the work in the project would be associated with modifications of the existing paperless settlement system, Talisman. Due to the tight deadlines it was envisaged that much of the new system would be created using a combination of external contractors and packaged software.

In October 1990 the SE published the business and technical specifications for Taurus. At around the same time it was revealed that a central component of the new Taurus system was to be a US-designed securities processing package VSPS. The decision to purchase VSPS at a cost of £2.2 million ($3.3 million) was taken in September 1990 once it was realized that there was insufficient time to complete an in-house system. As a result the in-house project to build a database system that had been in progress for around two years was abandoned and its staff transferred to work on Taurus.

The decision to purchase a standard packaged solution inevitably meant that the system would need to be modified to meet the

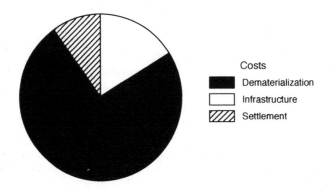

Figure 5.2 Breakdown of Taurus costs as at March 1990

Exchange's requirements. It was estimated that some 400 person-months of work would be required to tailor VSPS to meet the Taurus specifications, perhaps saving the Exchange many person-years of work overall. A team of 40 ´people, 25 located in Vista Concepts' New York base with the remainder in London, was established to modify the real-time Vista system, link it to the batch processing Talisman system and add the required Taurus-specific features. Vista Concepts were contracted to complete the modifications on the system on a time and materials basis. It was recognized at the time that the customization of VSPS would be the biggest challenge of the entire Taurus project.

The final architecture of the system, as illustrated in Figure 5.3, is a distributed database with the SE Taurus systems acting as the hub of a large X25 network. Over this network participants including brokers, banks, institutional investors, share registrars and custodians would be

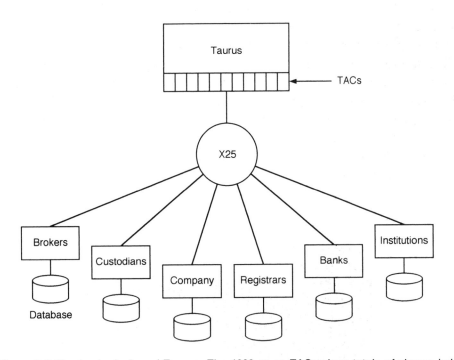

Figure 5.3 The basic design of Taurus. The 1000 or so TACs show totals of shares held by each participant institution that are available for BET to accounts of other participants. Individual ownership is not held. Individual ownership of shares (i.e. the full details of who owns which shares) will be held on a separate but linked database by each of the participant sites

connected both to the Taurus system and to each other. All share trading would take place over this network with transfer of ownership taking place electronically rather than by the movement of paper share certificates.

Each of the participants would maintain Taurus accounts in which the totals of each share that are held are shown. Information about ownership of shares would not be on Taurus itself. All shares were to be held under the name of the broker or other institution that was to control the account. The detailed information relating to individual share ownership was to be stored in a large number of separate databases operated by brokers, registrars, or listed companies themselves.

When shares were bought or sold the broker handling the trade would notify the deal to Taurus over the X25 network, together with information about where the shares were recorded and the transfer of ownership to wherever the buyer wished to keep his or her shares. The Taurus system would then transfer the appropriate number of shares between accounts. Periodically Taurus account holders were to notify company registrars of share transfers to enable them to update their records.

Although at this stage it was unknown how many institutions, banks and registrars would choose to participate in the system it was anticipated that the network would extend to over 400 locations and probably have to cope with a different combination of hardware and software at each site. It is worth noting that the SE had little prior experience of building a such a large and complex distributed database system.

The security aspects of this paperless system were considered too sensitive to be included in the business and technical specification that was published at this time. However, it was later revealed that the SE was to use IBM systems to ensure secure access to Taurus, as shown in Figure 5.4. The security system had three main elements, a security module running on a central IBM 3090 mainframe computer, a micro-computer-based secure key-registry system, and a large number of participant systems linked to the exchange. The security system was based on IBM's Data Encryption Standard (DES) and made use of smart cards and identification codes to ensure legitimate access to the system with all data transmissions being encrypted. This level of security was to ensure that only authorized users could trade using the system. The systems to

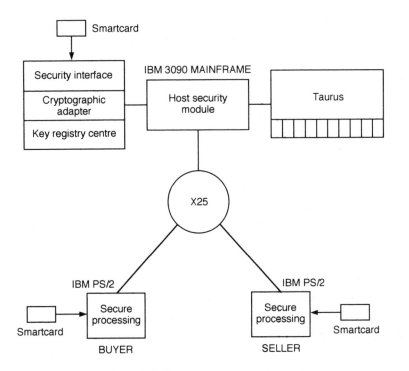

Figure 5.4 Taurus security systems

be used were said to make the network the most secure non–military computer system in the world.

The participant systems, IBM PS/2 microcomputers, were themselves designed to be very secure since they contained highly sensitive security software. Indeed, if there was an attempt to open up a system to gain access to the security chips, the chips were designed automatically to burn themselves out and thereby prevent the software from falling into the wrong hands.

The system was also designed to ensure that 'phantom transactions' could never occur. The IBM approach to what was called 'non–repudiation' meant that all transactions would be written to secure databases as they were made, ensuring that a full audit trail of transactions existed within the system.

The year 1991 started with the Project Director for Taurus announcing that implementation would be postponed from October 1991 until the first half of 1992. The major cause of this postponement was due to the complexity of the legal and regulatory changes that were necessary as the market moved to paperless trading. The SE, and the rest of the stock market, had to rely upon the Department of Trade and Industry (DTI) to write the new regulations that would have to pass through Parliament and become law before Taurus could begin operations. The regulations were issued, in draft form, on the same day as the delay to Taurus was announced.

Disputes over which organization, the SE or a government department, should oversee the operation of Taurus and the size of a new compensation fund to cover losses that could be caused by the system rumbled on through the first half of 1991. These were largely settled with the publication in May of a 152-page draft of the legal framework which was to govern the operation of Taurus.

In May 1991 the SE published a detailed timetable for the development, legislative and regulatory stages that had to be completed before the introduction of Taurus. This timetable (see Figure 5.5), largely determined by the legislation that needed to be passed through Parliament, predicted that the first stage of Taurus (paperless trading) would go live by the new date of 11 May 1992. The introduction of rolling settlement, the second stage (in which all deals were to be settled a set number of days after they were made), would now come into effect by the end of 1992.

1991

July	Information packs sent out to listed companies and shareholders. Final technical specification issued.
October	Legislation laid before Parliament
November	Publication of Taurus rules Parliament votes on Taurus legislation Shareholder compensation arrangements published

1992

February	Publication of costs to organizations using Taurus
March	Full trial begins for Taurus users
11 May	Taurus goes live
End 1992	introduction of rolling settlement and secure delivery against payment

Figure 5.5 May 1991 timetable for the introduction of Taurus

Just five months later, in September 1991, it emerged that it was doubtful that Taurus would meet the new target date of May 1992. A number of difficulties, including development problems associated with enhancing the existing settlement system Talisman, meant that the likely target date would be put back by several months. At the same time, it was also revealed that the published timetable had not included any slack and had been published purely to accelerate the pace of technical development within the securities industry.

October 1991 saw the publication of another new timetable for the introduction of Taurus, with April 1993 the new target date. Adding some £15 million ($22.5 million) to the original £50 million ($75 million) cost to the SE of the project, the new timetable assumed that regulations would be agreed with the government by November 1991, with final specifications being published shortly afterwards. Full testing was scheduled to commence in November 1992. This new timetable was produced as a result of consultation with securities firms and a thorough review of the systems development process involving the two main sub-contractors on the project, IBM and Vista.

At the close of the year the regulations necessary to provide the legal framework for Taurus were laid before Parliament. At the same time, the overall system was simplified as the proposal, originally included at government insistence, that every investor be issued with a 13-digit personal authorization code was dropped. The removal of this requirement, which would have meant that investors would have had to quote their authorization code before they could buy or sell shares, meant that one part of the system's complexity was eliminated.

After further delays, including the late delivery of the 'hacker-proof' security system, parts of the Taurus system began to emerge. In October 1992 large-scale testing began on the first phase of Taurus, the system that handled the settlement of shares sales. The testing was intended to take place in three stages, Entry Testing, Participant testing and Many-to-Many Testing. Entry testing involved the financial institutions linking up with the central Taurus computer and running their own systems on software designed to simulate live operations. Participant testing took this a stage further with the SE's own systems interacting directly with participants' systems. The final level of testing, Many-to-Many Testing, involved participants joining together to conduct trials between themselves through the central Taurus computer to ensure that the system worked as expected. It was only at the insistence of participant organizations that this final stage of Many-to-Many Testing was included in the overall programme. The addition of this last stage of testing was responsible for the implementation date for Taurus being moved to the first part of 1994.

In parallel with the Taurus software development dramatic upheavals were taking place within the rest of the SE information systems operation. After a three-month review by Andersen Consulting, the SE contracted with Andersen to run its entire IT operations for the next five years, resulting in a number of redundancies. Although the Taurus development project was excluded from the deal, Andersen was to be responsible for running the system when it went live.

In September 1992 Andersen, in preparation for the time when they would take over running of Taurus, undertook an examination of the system. Their report, submitted in December 1992, revealed the existence of a number of serious problems with Taurus. Fundamentally, it was found that there was no overall architecture for the Taurus system and it was suggested that it was unworkable.

In January 1993 a Coopers & Lybrand consultant, brought in to run the technical side of Taurus, ordered a full review of the project. This review revealed a series of problems that would take a long time to correct and would cause the testing programme to be postponed for at least 15 months. As a result of the review it was estimated that Taurus would take another three years to build and that costs could double. On 11 March 1993 the Board of the London Stock Exchange voted to abandon the Taurus project.

Causes of the Taurus Disaster

By the time the decision to abandon Taurus was made the cost to the SE of the development, subsequently to be written off, stood at some £75 million ($112 million). Estimates of the cost of the cancellation to the rest of the securities industry ranged between £200 million ($300 million) and £400 million ($600 million), with the software houses developing Taurus compliant systems also facing huge losses, resulting in at least one bankruptcy. On the day it was cancelled the 350 staff employed at the SE on the Taurus project lost their jobs.

Within a short time of the Taurus cancellation the SE declined to discuss the project and had archived all official documents. There was no official enquiry into the failure and authoritative reports on the project are not available. However, there was a great deal of comment and discussion in the specialist computing and financial press,[2] with some of the key players in the project giving off-the-record briefings. This information, while not definitive, provides a series of important clues that, taken with the known facts of the case, provide an insight into the progress of Project Taurus.

Origins of a Failure

The Taurus debacle has its origins in the arcane world of the London Stock Exchange and the powerful groups that work within it. The procedures of the SE with its two-week trading period go back to the pre-industrial days of horse travel and the time it took a rider to travel from London to York and back. This heritage, while in many ways a strength, has also impeded change and enabled individual interests to act against the interests of the long-term survival of the market as a whole.

The original Taurus design, based around a single centralized database, was pursued by the SE for the five years between 1983 and 1988 until it was scrapped as a result of pressure from within the market, as well as technical and financial problems. Given that the system would have taken over the work of the share registrars it is not surprising that the main pressure against the system came from these same registrars.

A market like the SE is a fragile thing and exists only because of the large number of financial institutions that wish to trade within it. The smooth running of the market depends upon gaining a balance between the interests of the powerful and influential institutions that makes up the market. As the SE found with the rejection of its original design for Taurus, it was not possible to propose a solution that ignored the interests of any significant part of that community.

---------........

[2] This section is based on Waters and Cane (1993), Waters (1993a–c), Green-Armytage (1993), Electronic Office (1993), Miles (1993), Willcock (1993), *The Economist* (1993, 1994), Peston (1993) and Penrose and McKenzie (1993).

Design by Committee

The establishment of a committee (Siscot) representing the major interests within the SE to develop a design that would be acceptable to all parts of the market appeared to be an ideal way forward. However, the creation of a committee to resolve a problem of this sort will usually have one of two outcomes. Either the members of the committee are willing to soften their demands in order produce a design that is a true compromise, or the members' interests are in such conflict that a compromise is not possible and the resulting design becomes an embodiment of that state of affairs. The design of Taurus was the result of the latter outcome, and was an attempt to avoid conflicting interests rather than meet multiple objectives. The result of this process was a highly complex design based around a distributed database linking computer systems at hundreds of sites, in stark contrast to the SE's original design for a single centralized database.

An unexpected side-effect of the committee approach to design was that, in response to pressure from one group or another, the specification of the system would have be changed. Registrars wanted to retain their role within the stock market, companies wanted to ensure they could track share ownership, brokers wanted to be able to avoid the costs of maintaining records of share ownership, the government were determined to protect the rights of small shareholders, with the SE wanting to get on with the job. All these, sometimes conflicting, interests made for a tortuous design process that produced a highly complex system.

Perhaps more important is the fact that complexities were added to the system as the development progressed, with the likely result being extensive reworking of the parts of the system that had already been designed or completed. A typical example of this was the insistence by the government that all personal shareholders be issued with a 13-digit id code that would allow them to authenticate their share trading. This idea was first proposed in May 1991, when development was supposedly well advanced, only to be abandoned in favour of a simpler written authorization in December later the same year. Such changes inevitably place a strain upon a development team who, given the lack of a complete design, may have found it easier to accede to the many changes that were requested. Not only was a full design of the system never completed but, in response to pressure from the users, testing of parts of the system had commenced while central parts of it were still unwritten.

Modifying the VSPS Package

The decision in 1990 to purchase and modify the US-designed Vista package rather than continue with an in-house development was also the source of many problems. If major modifications are likely to be necessary to a software package it is often a safer route to build a bespoke system and, while the risks of this approach were recognized, the decision proved to be a poor one.

Vista was designed to comply with US regulations and operate in an on-line environment. In order to be able to operate within the UK context and interface with the batch processing Talisman system the Vista system required major modifications, with some 70% of the system needing to be changed. The split between the two parts of the development team was also far from ideal, with communication between the sites apparently being poor. The continual changes made to the system specification may only have compounded an already difficult task. When the project was abandoned the cost of the still-unfinished modifications was £14 million ($21 million), an amount that can only have been inflated by the constantly changing requirements and the fact that all work by Vista Concepts was on a time and materials basis rather than on a fixed-price contract.

Receding Deadlines

The shifting nature of the system requirements inevitably had a knock-on effect for the final implementation dates, with deadlines being extended significantly at least six times over the life of the project, as illustrated in Figure 5.6. Repeatedly moving the implementation date is not only likely to erode the credibility of the system itself but also the likelihood that any future deadline will be achieved. Credibility is further undermined when it is admitted that such deadlines that have been announced have little or no slack and are intended purely to 'create a focus to force the rest of the [financial] industry to accelerate its technical development'[3].

[3] John Watson quoted in *Financial Times* (1991).

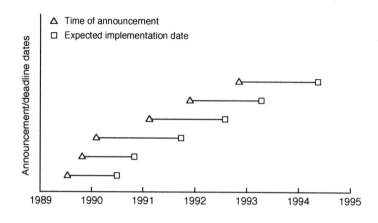

Figure 5.6 Constantly receding deadlines

Organizational Disruption

The end of 1989 was the beginning of a period of tremendous upheaval within the SE. In 1989 the SE employed around 3000 staff and was governed by a network of something like 90 committees and sub-committees. By 1993 the headcount had been reduced to around 1400 and number of committees to 16. In 1992 all IT operations, except for the Taurus development, had been outsourced to Andersen Consulting with the result that staff numbers were reduced still further.

Senior management oversight of the project was limited in that members of important committees charged with overseeing the progress were unwilling or unable to discover the true state of the development. One of these committees, the Taurus Monitoring Group, contained individuals with wide experience in developing financial systems but only met for 90 minutes a month—far too short a time to gain anything other than a superficial oversight of development.

Lessons of the Taurus Experience

At the heart of the Taurus fiasco are the issues surrounding the design, organizational, human-factor and financial aspects. We will now examine each aspect in turn.

System Design Lessons

The design for Taurus started out as a re-engineered system based on a relatively straightforward centralized database, but ended up replicating the existing inefficient structures within a complex distributed database system. While the original design was ostensibly rejected for technical reasons, the fact that it threatened a number of established City interests was probably the true source of the objections. Also the fact that, in the face of strong opposition, the SE pursued such a design for over five years illustrates the dangers of over-concentration, at an early stage, on technical rather than structural issues.

Taurus is a good illustration of the dangers of designing an information system by committee. The committee in question, Siscot, was made up of representatives of a range of powerful bodies with conflicting interests. However, the chair of the committee (the SE itself) had little or no power to direct events. In addition, since the various interest groups represented on the committee stood to gain little or nothing from a compromise solution, compromise was unnecessary and a solution could only be agreed if it was acceptable to all members. The result of developing a design under these conditions was to create a system that became increasingly complex as it replicated more and more of the existing structural inefficiencies. This emphasis on preserving existing systems and protecting entrenched interests meant that technology was used as a means of wish-fulfilment rather than a method of creating an efficient system.

The desire of the SE to keep control of the project and retain their position within the City of London meant that while, practically, they should have turned to an outside arbiter to offer guidance, politically they could not do so. This unwillingness to involve the UK government or the Bank of England led to the existing structural inefficiencies being designed into the new system, and contributed to the failure of the project.

The nature of the design process and the breadth of the committee membership meant that it became impossible to prevent changes being proposed as the development progressed. A prime example of this was the UK government's proposal in May 1991, some seven months after the publication of the technical specification, that personal shareholders be issued with a 13-digit id code. Intended as a secure means of enabling the many millions of personal shareholders to authenticate their share dealings, this proposal added yet another layer of complexity to an already over-complex design. Yet this proposal related far more to the UK government's political agenda than to the aim of achieving a workable system.

Organizational Lessons

The organizational issues are not quite so straightforward and involve the difficult problems of oversight and management. While delegation of authority is essential within any large organization, systems that monitor progress must also exist if senior management is to retain any kind of control at all over what is actually taking place. Until the summer of 1989, some two years after it had commenced, Taurus did not have an overall project director. This large project (it was said to be the largest software project in Europe involving some 300 person-years of work) was in fact managed through a network of over 20 committees.

The complexity of both the project and the committee structures must have presented a great challenge to creating an efficient reporting system that would have enabled senior managers to retain a feel for the progress of the project. Such a reporting structure would have been further undermined if those committees were unable (due to limitations on time or expertise) to confirm the accuracy of the information with which they were presented. The fact that there was no overall architecture for the system was only known by those 'at the heart of the project',[4] and senior managers outside the project were apparently unaware of the problems with the system.

Splitting development over two sites geographically remote from each other, as in the London/New York split of the VSPS development team, may lead to communication problems. Extensive and frequently used electronic communications are no substitute for meeting face to face.

The use of external advisors may be one way to provide the most senior management with a method of determining the true state of a project. However, while many consultants had worked on the project it was only after a review by Andersen Consulting that severe doubts about it were raised—some three years after it had commenced.

———— ....

[4] Sir Andrew Hugh Smith, chairman of the SE, speaking at the announcement of the cancellation of the Taurus project, quoted in Waters (1993c).

Human Lessons

The biggest challenge that faces organizations and individuals in projects like Taurus is how to keep a grip on reality. Project teams need to have a firm belief in their mission and that it is achievable. However, there is a risk that this belief can turn into blind faith as a project progresses and difficulties emerge. Announcing the cancellation of the project, Sir Andrew Hugh Smith said that 'there may have been an element of self-delusion' (quoted in *Financial Times*, 1993) among the project team that stopped them from recognizing the scale of the problems with the system at an early stage of the development.

The danger of any IS project is that it becomes too technology focused and ignores the wider organizational and political issues that surrounds the development. Taurus suffered from delays as a result of the tortuous process of drafting the legislation necessary to enable paperless trading to take place, yet surely this should have been anticipated and allowed for by those leading the project. Similarly, the original Taurus proposal of a single central database was a technology-led solution that ignored the many established interests within the stock market. That the SE persisted with this proposal for so long was to result in much wasted time and effort.

Financial Lessons

Taurus was a 'must-do' project. Given its international competition the SE felt it had no choice but to move to paperless trading. The cost–benefit analysis for the Taurus project which was only completed in 1990 once the final design had emerged revealed that the system would save the City of London over £250 million ($375 million) over ten years and would cost between £45 million and £50 million ($67.5–75 million). In the event it cost the SE itself £75 million ($112.5 million), the other financial organisations involved £200–400 million ($300–600 million) and saved the City of London nothing at all.

Such detailed cost–benefit calculations as were prepared at the start of the project are worth little if they are not continually updated as development progresses. If this is done it becomes possible to determine both the true cost and worth of a system. If this is not done development becomes an act of faith rather than an informed decision.

A major problem for the Taurus development was the use of time and materials contracts with many of the contractors who worked on the project. The cost escalation of the Vista modifications from £4 million to £14 million ($6–21 million) is an example of what such contracts can lead to. However, it also demonstrates that it was unlikely that the complexity of the task was fully understood by either side when the contract was signed. A fixed-price contract will inevitably impose discipline on both sides. The supplier must understand and cost the problem and the requirements in great detail, and the purchaser must also understand what they have agreed with the supplier. This apparently balanced equation does, however, need detailed recalculation if the system requirements change.

VARIATIONS ON A THEME

There have been many cases over the years of where the development of computer-based financial systems that have gone badly wrong although few, for obvious reasons, ever make the headlines. One that did is the MasterNet system.

The Bank of America and MasterNet[5]

The abandonment of MasterNet by the Bank of America (B of A) early in 1988 marked the end of a disastrous attempt to create a leading-edge system that cost the bank over $80 million (£53 million) and resulted in the closure of its trust business. The saga of MasterNet started with the decision some six years earlier to create an advanced new system that would enable B of A to become a major player in the trust business. At that time the bank's trust business—managing the complex investment and property portfolios on behalf of large corporations, government agencies and individuals—was comparatively modest, and the recent in-house attempt to upgrade the existing system had cost $6 million (£4 million) and ended in failure. The MasterNet system, to be developed by the specialist software house Premier Systems, was to be a key

_____ ....
[5] This case is based on Frantz (1988) and *Los Angeles Times* (1987, 1988).

component in a larger $4 billion (£2.7 billion) strategy to use technology to place the B of A at the leading edge of technology. The champion of this strategy was the CEO of the BankAmerica parent company.

The risk of developing the $20 million (£14 million) MasterNet was to be shared by a consortium made up of the B of A and three smaller banks, Seattle-First National Bank, United Virginia Bank and Philadelphia National Bank. After a period of extensive research, the funding for the project was approved and Premier Systems began work in March 1984, with B of A staff working in parallel on a suite of eight smaller systems called TrustPlus that were intended to extend MasterNet's functionality.

Great care was taken throughout the systems analysis and design stages of the project and the creation of what was a highly complex system proceeded slowly. The scale of the development can be demonstrated by the fact that MasterNet contained some 3.5 million lines of code, and that some 20 person-years to testing were undertaken by the B of A in order to test the new system in addition to the 13 000 hours of training that was given to the users.

By May 1986 the B of A were happy enough with the new system to hold a two-day preview for the bank's most important trust clients. The event was a great success and the corporate clients were promised that they would soon be able to convert to the new system, although the reality was that new bugs were still being found and MasterNet was not considered reliable enough for clients to be moved over from the old system. The corporate clients began to be restive and looked for signs of progress. This was a time of great pressure on the bank's staff since both the old and new trust systems were being operated in parallel, with the result that many staff were working extremely long hours. The work on the MasterNet system throughout 1986 was taking place against a background of large losses and retrenchment, with parts of the business being sold off and 9600 jobs being cut. The major sponsor and supporter of the MasterNet system was one of those who left the organization.

Finally, the new system seemed stable enough to move to final conversion. However, in the final run-in to the conversion date of 2 March 1987 half the team was pulled off to work on another project. Despite this setback the conversion went ahead and the system successfully went live, although it went down again five days later when one of its 24 disk drives blew up, causing part of the main database to be lost. The database was successfully rebuilt using backup data, and even though such a problem had not occurred during system testing, over the next four weeks around 14 more of the disk drives blew up. At the same time as the systems team was struggling with this crisis, it was announced that it had been decided to move the data processing headquarters some 30 miles away in order to cut costs. This event became a focus for discontent, causing some staff to leave and adversely affecting the morale of those who remained.

But these were not the only problems that affected the MasterNet system, since it had become apparent that key parts of TrustPlus were not working correctly. One of the important roles of the TrustPlus was to reconcile the large amount of securities trading that takes place within any trust system, posting each of the transactions to the correct accounts and enabling the securities group to agree the records of the brokers who made the trades. Fundamentally TrustPlus could not do this, with the effect that the securities group were solely relying on information from outside brokers in order to settle transactions. This was an appalling situation for the securities group to be in and led to their resistance to, and a lack of cooperation with, the new system. This situation, combined with plans to move the securities operation from Los Angeles to San Francisco, made an already bad situation much worse. As a result of these problems nearly 40 staff were to leave the organization and large numbers of temporary staff were employed at great cost to sort out the reconciliation problems. Throughout this period the bank's customer service deteriorated and certainly did not live up to the impressive vision demonstrated in 1986. Corporate clients began to withdraw their business, eventually resulting in the loss of around 100 accounts representing $4 billion (£2.7 billion) worth of assets.

In July 1987 it was disclosed that $25 million (£17 million) had been set aside to cover losses that were expected to arise due to problems with the MasterNet system. It also emerged that the bank was looking for a buyer for its trust business, and that an in-house inquiry into the MasterNet/TrustPlus system had been started, eventually resulting in the resignations of managers involved with the project. In January 1988 it was announced that a further $35 million (£24 million) was to be set aside to correct problems with the system, with the effect that some $60 million (£40 million) had been allocated to fix a system that cost $20 million (£14 million) to create. Eventually the bank threw in the towel and abandoned its trust business, transferring the majority of its clients to another bank in the BankAmerica group and giving the remaining accounts away. Costing the B of A a total of $80 million (£54 million), the whole episode had proved an expensive and embarrassing disaster.

References

The Economist, 'When the bull turned', 20 March (1993).

The Economist, 'London's Taurus nightmare', 13 March (1994).

Electronic Office, 'Lessons of Taurus,' 17 March, 2 (1993).

Financial Times, 'Taurus system likely to miss target date', 16 September, 1 (1991).

Financial Times, 'Angry City takes stock of lost time and money', 12 March, 11 (1993).

Frantz, D., 'B of A's plans for computer don't add up', *Los Angeles Times*, 8 February (1988).

Green-Armytage, J., 'Why Taurus was always ill-starred', *Computer Weekly*, 18 March, 10 (1993).

Los Angeles Times, '$23 million computer snafu adds to B of A's troubles', 24 July (1987).

Los Angeles Times, 'B of A abandons costly computer for trust clients', 26 January (1988).

Miles, R., Death in the afternoon for Taurus', *Computing*, 18 March, 7 (1993).

Penrose, P. and McKenzie, H., 'Recriminations fly as Taurus is scrapped', *Banking Technology*, April, 4 (1993).

Peston, R., 'Stock Exchange chief failed to tame bull', *Financial Times*, 12 March, 11 (1993).

Waters, R., 'Harsh post-mortem reveals flaws', *Financial Times* 19 March, 11 (1993a).

Waters, R., 'The plan that fell to earth', *Financial Times*, 12 March, 19 (1993b).

Waters, R., 'Stock market chief quits over Taurus', *Financial Times*, 12 March, 1 (1993c).

Waters, R., 'Stock Exchange takes a matador to Taurus', *Financial Times*, 11 March, 11 (1993d).

Waters, R. and Cane, A., 'Sudden death of a runaway bull', *Financial Times*, 19 March, 11 (1993).

Willcock, J., 'The City comes unplugged', *The Independent on Sunday*, 14 March, 4 (1993).

GOVERNMENT
COMPUTER PROJECTS

. . . .

Making government more effective and efficient is a national issue.
But getting it to work better and cost less will be impossible if
federal agencies cannot learn to manage with modern practices the
information age demands.[1]

. . . .

[1] Charles A. Bowsher, Comptroller General of the United States, writing in the preface to GAO (1994).

This chapter discusses the specific nature of government IS developments and examines a range of IS failures in both the UK and the USA. Using authoritative government reports as a basis, the progress of several IS projects is recorded and the factors contributing to their subsequent failure analysed. A range of lessons relevant to the conduct of all IS developments is drawn.

Introduction

Governments spend billions[2] a year acquiring new technology and many millions more running their current systems, making them probably the largest users of information technology. They are not, however, always the most effective or successful users of technology and there are many examples of government computer systems that have failed in the most spectacular fashion. This chapter will provide a brief look at some of the most interesting recent cases and attempt to extract the useful management lessons that can be learnt from them.

The three major cases—the Wessex RISP system, The Field System and Veterans Benefits Administration—represent two failures and a very near miss. Together they demonstrate clusters of problems that could equally have occurred within commercial systems development, and for this reason the lessons drawn will be of general applicability.

The small cases included are intended to underline the lessons of the larger ones and serve to demonstrate the scale of the problems that governments have encountered in attempting to make good use of new technology.

Are Government Computer Projects Different?

In attempting to provide an answer to this question we will be looking first at the characteristics of the information systems government must create to handle their information problems, before examining how these systems are actually realized.

Government computer systems often appear superficially to be very

---

[2] In 1993 spending stood at around £2 billion ($3 billion) in the UK and $20 billion (£13.3 billion) in the USA.

similar to commercial developments. The truth is, however, that while they might use similar technology or even do similar things, government systems generally belong to the information system superleague. The very nature of the tasks national governments have to undertake on our behalf, administering the tax and benefit systems for example, inevitably means that the information systems that are developed to deal with these tasks bear little resemblance to standard commercial systems. Government information systems can be said to differ from commercial systems in five major respects:

- *Size* Government information systems are often intended to serve national or regional populations of many millions of people with the result that the volumes of data dealt with are huge.
- *One-offs* Applications tend to be unique, with the result that the government is forced to create its own systems rather than purchase them ready-made. The many differences in law and government systems between nations merely serves to underline the one-off nature of the systems that must be created.
- *Complexity* The systems that governments must create will have at their core complex legislation that provides an underlying definition of its purpose. This core set of requirements is often the result of a body of legislation that has built up over the years. When combined with the requirements necessary to operationalize, this inevitably produces systems of awesome complexity.
- *Very long development timescale* The scale of government operations and speed with which they are able to bring about changes mean that the development of new computer systems is likely to be very protracted.
- *Very high cost* Government information systems are thus likely to be very large-scale developments which, due to their unique nature, require custom solutions with highly complex requirements that result in very long development times. This can only mean one thing: a very high price tag.

The areas that best illustrate these five differences are the developments surrounding the core governmental systems of taxation and social security. In the USA since its commencement in 1986 the Internal Revenue Service (IRS) has been engaged in a Tax System Modernization programme whose aim is to create a fully automated and modernized tax-processing system. In the four years to 1990 the IRS spent around $120 million (£80 million) on the project which is expected to have a final cost of $23 billion (£15.3 billion) and last until the year 2008, making it one of the largest civilian computer projects in history.

In the UK the plan to computerize the social security benefit system, called the Operational Strategy, was begun in 1982 and was largely completed by 1993. The cost of realizing the Operational Strategy was originally estimated to be some £570 million ($855 million), although by 1993 this had risen to something like £2 billion ($3 billion)[3]. The USA has a similar programme but, despite having identified 23 major areas within its operation that required work, by 1991 it had still to complete an Agency Strategic plan to define the long-term structure and vision of its modernization programme.

The process of building the large and complex information systems required by government is also likely to be very different from the creation of the majority of commercial information systems. While some of the factors listed below may apply to some commercial projects, most of them could be applied to the majority of government computer projects that have taken place:

1. *Technology-led*   There has been a tendency for government information systems to be technology-led rather than oriented more towards the satisfaction of the needs of the public whom it is intended to serve. In this sense they are often not 'customer-facing', in the commercial sense of the term, since there is no fear that the customers—the public—will take their 'business' elsewhere.

2. *Low-cost solutions not sought*   The preference for solutions that make use of leading-edge technologies within government projects indicates that there may be a tendency to adopt high-cost approaches to systems, rather than take a low-cost solution.

3. *Custom systems rather than packaged solutions preferred*   The unique nature of many of the core governmental information systems has

---————........

[3] Estimates vary from the official figure of £1.8 billion ($2.4 billion) to unofficial estimates that indicate the final figure to be £2 billion ($3 billion), or even as high as £2.6 billion ($3.9 billion). It is in fact difficult to establish the exact cost of implementing the Operational Strategy due to organizational restructuring and the dispersion of costs throughout the Department IT budget as a whole.

tended to throw a shadow over all other information systems developments. There may thus be a tendency to assume that all government information systems would thus require a custom rather than packaged solution.

4. *Short-term tenures of managers overseeing projects* Continuity of the management overseeing large information systems developments is essential. However, management changes have been a feature of many government information systems developments, with adverse affects upon their focus and progress.

5. *Priorities may be refocused* Changes in government policy towards the organization and provision of public services occurring in the middle of an information systems development are likely to have severe implications for its progress.

6. *Imposition of external deadlines* A component of any change in government policy is likely to be a date, generally selected primarily for political reasons, by which changes will take place. Such dates then become the deadlines by which information systems must be operational.

7. *Highly bureaucratic decision-making processes* The level of oversight within government is a component of the need to ensure the highest level of accountability for the use of public funds. This system to ensure financial probity, together with arcane public budgeting procedures, very often has the effect of creating organizational structures unsuited to the effective management of information systems projects.

8. *High level of public interest and oversight* Government computer projects are carried out in the public arena surrounded by a level of interest and access that is generally unknown in the commercial world. The amount of information that may become available on the process as well as the outcome of a government project is far higher than for commercial projects which, whatever the outcome, are generally shrouded in secrecy.

These points can be illustrated by reference to a few of the many information systems projects that the UK and USA governments have undertaken in recent years. The Veterans Benefits system, the Wessex RISP system and The Field System (all of which are discussed below) are prime examples of technology-led developments in which low-cost solutions were not fully considered. The Field System is also an example in which there was a decision to develop custom software when packaged software could arguably have provided an equal level of functionality at much lower cost.

The impact of management changes and the subsequent refocusing of priorities can also be seen in the Wessex RISP case and appears to have been a major problem affecting US government projects[4], a prime example of this being Social Security Administration (SSA) in the USA (GAO, 1991a). Between 1973 and 1991 the SSA had ten commissioners, each of whom served for an average of 2–3 years, with four serving a total of just 47 months between them. The implications of these repeated changes in senior management was that the SSA was restructured in 1975, 1979, 1983 and 1990, and the agency's technology strategy (the Systems Modernization Plan) was revised four times between its creation in 1982 and its demise in 1988. The Systems Modernization Plan was replaced by 'SSA 2000: A Strategic Plan' in 1988, which itself was replaced by the 'Information Systems Plan' in 1991. None of the plans listed above were in existence long enough to be able to fully achieve their objectives.

The problems of externally imposed deadlines are amply illustrated in The Field System case (see below), with another example (also in the UK) being the Poll Tax/Council Tax developments. Within the space of the four years between 1989 and 1993 local government in the UK had to develop and implement, against tight externally set deadlines, two entirely separate taxation systems as first the Poll Tax was introduced, only to be abolished and replaced within a few years by the Council Tax.

The cumbersome administrative processes that often surround government information systems and the poor oversight that can sometimes result are amply demonstrated in the cases examined throughout this chapter.

———— ....

[4] A series of reports from the General Accounting Office have all made this point. The lack of detailed information makes it impossible to know how much this problem also affects UK government projects.

Problems with Government Computer Projects

The fact that government computer projects are open to far greater public scrutiny that commercial systems is illustrated in the succession of reports issued by, in the UK, the National Audit Office (NAO) and, in the USA the General Accounting Office (GAO). The reports by these two organizations (and in the UK the public hearing conducted by the Public Accounts Committee) provide an often detailed (and highly critical) insight into the conduct of government departments and their systems development efforts.

In 1992 the GAO produced a summary report that reviewed all of the reports prepared by its Information Management Technology Division between 1988 and 1991 (GAO, 1992a). Of the 192 reports that had been prepared nearly 70% (132) identified one or more problems related to information resources management (IRM[5]). The summary is shown in Table 6.1. Of the ten categories examined it can be seen that the top four problems they identified were:

1. Inadequate management of information systems lifecycle
2. Ineffective oversight and control of IRM
3. Cost overruns
4. Schedule delays

It is very likely that these problems could equally apply to information systems being developed by UK government departments, as the London Ambulance Service and Field System cases illustrate.

While the NAO has not produced anything like as comprehensive a view of UK government projects, a summary report was published in 1990 that examined the management of computer projects in the National Health Service (NHS) (National Audit Office, 1990). Table 6.2 shows the NAO's assessment of how well each project complied with standards of good practice across five categories. It is notable that the bulk of the projects examined were judged to be either inadequate or poor across all five categories.

---------........

[5] This has been defined as 'the planning, budgeting, organizing, directing, training, promoting, controlling and other managerial activities involved with the collection or creation, use, and dissemination of information'.

Table 6.1 Number of reports citing information resources management problems

Problem	Numbers of reports for fiscal year			Total[b]
	1989	1990	1991[a]	
Inadequate management of information systems development life cycle	24	33	9	66
Ineffective oversight and control of IRM	7	18	4	29
Inability to ensure the security, integrity or reliability of information systems	3	11	2	16
Inability of systems to work together	2	8	4	14
Inadequate resources to accomplish IRM goals	2	5	2	9
Cost overruns	13	6	3	22
Schedule delays	10	8	2	20
Systems not performing as intended	3	3	1	7
Data that were inaccurate, unreliable, or incomplete	4	7	7	18
Systems that make access to data time-consuming or cumbersome	2	4	2	8

[a]Fiscal year 1991 reports include only those issued before 31 May, 1991.
[b]Reports that identified more than one problem are listed under more than one category, so the total number of reports is more than 132.
Source: Stock Exchange prepares traders for paperless settlement, *Financial Times*, 10 March, 1990.

Table 6.2 National Audit Office assessment of compliance with good practice

Feature of good practice	Number of projects assessed as:			
	Good	Adequate	Inadequate	Poor
Feasibility studies	–	4	4	3
Contract arrangements	1	4	3	3
Planning	–	3	4	4
Project management and control	–	4	4	3
Post-implementation review[a]	–	1	2	6
Totals	1	16	17	19

[a]Assessment excludes two projects not yet complete.
Source: NAO (1990. Crown copyright).

The Cases

The three major cases in this section all represent different types of computer project, planned at different times by different government departments in different countries. However, as we will see, similar mistakes were made and similar lessons can be drawn from each project. The major difference between them all is that one was stopped before things had gone too far, and thus is presented as a 'near-miss' rather than an information systems disaster.

The Wessex Regional Information Systems Plan[6]

Not an Educated Client[7]

This case is an example of a grandiose computerization scheme that became, five years and £43 million ($64.5 million) after it had started, a major public scandal. While much of the scandal surrounding the Wessex Regional Information Systems Plan was linked to dubious commercial and management practices and financial fraud, this case will confine itself to an examination of the conception and management of the computerization project itself.[8]

At the time of the RISP development Wessex Regional Health Authority, part of the UK NHS, was responsible for the provision of healthcare for a major part of Southern England. The Regional Health

———— . . . .

[6] The details in this case are sourced from: Committee of Public Accounts (1993) and National Audit Office (1990).

[7] This is based on a comment by the Regional General Manager of Wessex RHA to the Public Accounts Committee. In explaining the comment he went on to say: 'I think I need just to explain the term "educated client" in the way that I have used it. . . . What I mean is that I believe any public authority needs to have available to it expert advice which is retained by it, which owes no loyalty to anybody else, which is not involved in tendering for work and which can advise it on the specification of the work to be done. That by itself is certainly not enough. Then you need to go on to have proper financial and procurement procedures. You need to have proper project management. You need to undertake these big projects if you are going to do it at all, in bite sized chunks, you need to have effective non-executive scrutiny and, . . . you must abide by the well-established . . . rules and values in relation to conflicts of interest. That clearly was not the case in Wessex.'

[8] Those wishing to examine this case in detail are recommended to refer to the PAC report referenced above. This report is over 200 pages in length and provides a detailed insight into the conduct surrounding the project. The Wessex episode also provoked an enormous amount of press comment during the PAC hearings and after the publication of the report in late 1993.

Authority (RHA) was divided into ten Districts, each of which was in turn responsible for the provision of healthcare for its local area.

The origins of RISP (Regional Information Systems Plan)[9] go back to 1982 when the decision was made to develop an information systems strategy that would cover all information requirements within the entire Wessex RHA. The origins for this concept can be traced to the recognition by senior managers within Wessex RHA of the need to coordinate IT developments, and to an IBM management course attended by staff from Wessex during which the need for new-style integrated information systems was discussed.

The feasibility study undertaken at a very early stage of the project set out to identify information requirements (using the IBM Business Systems Planning methodology) identified five major core systems that would form the basis for an all-embracing system:

- Accountancy
- Manpower
- Hospital
- Estates
- Community

RISP was intended to create a totally integrated information system. All applications would be accessible from any terminal on the network, and data held by any individual program could also be accessed by any other application.

In May 1984 RISP was formally adopted by Wessex Regional Health Authority, its aim being described as: 'To use modern technology in order to optimize the use of information in the continuing improvement of the effectiveness and efficiency of clinical and other health services' (Committee of Public Accounts, 1993). The main points of the plan were as follows:

- The development of five major systems in every district of the region operating to common standards
- The development to be completed within five years

---

[9] RISP originally stood for Regional Information Strategy Project. This was changed to Regional Information Systems Plan in 1984.

- A transitional strategy to make use of existing systems, provided they worked well and could be integrated with RISP
- RISP was to developed centrally by Wessex RHA, although the operational responsibilities for systems were to be passed on to the Districts.

The cost and scale of the development were both significant. Officially the capital cost of the plan (at 1984–5 prices) was put at £26 million ($39 million), with an additional £17.5 million ($26 million) in revenue costs being incurred over the life of the project. Official estimates also stated that the system would require 500 person-years of programming which, given the small number of staff available to work on the project, would mean a significant input from external consultants.

The following sections are intended to provide an overview of the main aspects of the progress of the RISP development.

Management Oversight of the Project

Over the life of the project external auditors presented a series of reports that were critical of various aspects of the project. These reports, covering development and procurement procedures, financial control, use of contract staff, purchase of computers and project management, appeared to have had little impact upon the progress of the project. On the basis of these reports the Management Executive of the NHS had raised a series of points with the RHA concerning many aspects of the project. However, no significant action was taken to correct the fundamental problems with the project.

The Procurement Process

One hallmark of this case is the number of occasions in which an apparent conflict of interest arose in the procurement process.

In February 1986 Digital Equipment Corporation (DEC) was selected, out of a total of five proposals, as the preferred supplier of hardware for the project. The RHA then informed the four losers of the tendering process, including the Andersen Consulting/IBM consortium that, although not on the preferred list, they were not to be excluded from the tendering process. Four months later Andersen Consulting were appointed to advise on the selection of software suppliers for the DEC-based system. In August 1986 the RHA requested the original tenderers to confirm and update their proposals and one month later, at an inquorate meeting of the RHA's Information Group, it was decided to award the contract for the hardware and the software to the Andersen Consulting/IBM consortium. The contract did not contain any quality provisions and did not specify a maximum price.

In March 1989 the decision was taken to purchase (without going out to tender) an IBM 3090 computer[10] for £3.3 million ($5 million), the contract including an option to cancel that was valid until January 1990. In September 1989 the RHA took delivery of the mainframe computer, although by this time it could have been purchased for as little as £2.3 million ($3.45 million). By the time the computer was actually brought into use in March 1991 its estimated value had declined to around £1 million ($1.5 million).

Other Problems with the Development

There were a great many problems within the RISP development, and the following selection should provide a flavour of their scale:

- *Lack of a clear definition of the scope of RISP* The boundaries of the RISP system were never clearly defined, leading to difficulties in budgeting and controlling expenditure of the project. The 'official' 1983 estimate for the development of the five core systems was put at between £24 million and £33 million ($36–50 million), with this estimate to rise by a further £8 million ($12 million) if consultants were to be employed. Internal unofficial estimates of the project were that it would cost not less than £80 million ($120 million) (Committee of Public Accounts, 1993).
- *Management of the project* RISP was a technology-led project that, in the words of the PAC report, 'was pursued in the face of the good practical evidence that it was not working out'. That same document reports that within Wessex senior management there was a 'near-obsessional belief' in RISP.
- *Project management* It appears that a full project plan was never

———————........

[10] It was later to be revealed that the additional capacity provided by the mainframe computer was not required.

developed and that projects within RISP were authorized on an *ad-hoc* basis such that the development plan tended to evolve over time. Once projects had been given approval it was the responsibility of an RHA official to sign-off the project once it was completed. However, the sizing of projects was generally undertaken by the external consultants without the involvement of RHA officials, thereby leaving the RHA reliant on these same external consultants for all project management.

- *Poor supervision of consultant's work* Of the 158 projects carried out by external consultants many lacked formal definition and many seem to have been based on verbal agreement reached at informal meetings.
- *Poor financial control* Detailed budgets were not calculated before the start of the financial year and were set at aggregate levels, often in millions of pounds. IT budget holders had little control over the production or management of their budgets, wrongly assuming that this was undertaken by the Finance Function within the RHA.

By time RISP was abandoned in April 1990 some £43 million ($64.5 million) had been spent on the project. The main achievements of the project on the five core systems were as follows:

1. *Estates* No working systems were produced (although a standard package was installed)
2. *Hospital* Only one hospital implemented the information system, with a second to follow. Two other Districts abandoned plans to use system after £1.8 million ($2.7 million) in licence fees and consultancy had been spent.
3. *Finance* General Ledger was provided to all Districts and Accounts Payable in five Districts. The Purchasing system was rejected in favour of existing systems.
4. *Personnel* Expenditure of £1.6 million ($2.4 million) was incurred before the system was abandoned. No working systems installed.
5. *Community* Feasibility study completed (costing £188 000 ($282 000)), system then abandoned.

In addition to the above a number of smaller systems were introduced.

The end result of the RISP project was that Wessex RHA still did not have the information systems that they perceived as essential to the effective management of their operations. Of the £43 million ($64.5 million) the project cost it was estimated that at least £20 million ($30 million) of this amount was wasted.

The Field System[11]

I do not see this as a debacle, but as a partial success.[12]

This case examines the history of a system that was built by one organization (the Department of Employment), on behalf of others (the Training and Education Councils or TECs), was largely rejected by its intended users once installed, and then ceased to be supported just seven months after the last of the TECs started to use it. All at a cost to the taxpayer of £48 million ($72 million).

The origins of the development go back to a 1988 review report by the Department of Employment into the systems operating within its regional offices. The review recommended that the five separate systems that had evolved over the years should be replaced with a single integrated system run on distributed minicomputers that would supply the needs of each field office. The review expected that the new system would be more usable and produce better-quality information to improve decision making. It was recognized in this review that the new system would be at the leading edge of developments and would be a technically high-risk project. This new system, now called The Field System (TFS), was planned to be implemented between June 1990 and April 1992.

At the end of 1988 the government announced the establishment of Training and Education Councils (TECs). The TECs were to be commercial organizations, independent of the government, that were to take over the work of the Department of Employment's field offices. At this stage it was not known how many TECs there were likely to be nor how fast they would come into operation. However, the develop-

---........

[11] The details of the case are sourced from National Audit Office (1993) and Committee of Public Accounts (1994).
[12] This is a quote from a statement made by Mr Monck, a senior government official in The Department of Employment, whilst giving evidence to the Committee of Public Accounts.

ment of the new information system for the offices due to be replaced—The Field System—was already under way.

The business case prepared for TFS assumed that it would be necessary to provide the new TECs with a common information system rather than allow them to determine their own needs. It was also decided that the only practical option available was to provide a redesigned version of The Field System that was then under development.

The Business Case, which estimated the cost of TFS to be some £71 million ($106.5 million), compared two choices—development of TFS or the upgrade of the existing systems. Other options, use by TECs of manual systems until they were in a position to determine their own needs or the development of an entirely new system, were not considered. One of the anticipated benefits of TFS was that it would provide the flexibility and resilience required to meet future needs and adapt to changing requirements. However, the many risks surrounding the decision to adapt TFS—a system originally conceived for internal departmental use—were not considered in the Business Case. The uncertainties ignored by the Business Case included the following risks:

- The information needs of both the TECs and the Department were likely to change during the development of TFS.
- The information needs of the TECs would have to be defined by the Department as, at this time, none had been set up.
- The information needs would be likely to vary between TECs as each would be a separate commercial organization delivering services to their local areas.
- It was not known how many TECs there would be.
- It was not known how fast the TECs would come into being as they were permitted to become operational as soon as they were ready.
- TFS would need to be ready six months earlier than originally planned in order to coincide with the expected timetable for the move over to the TECs.

In August 1989 the proposal to build TFS received the go-ahead and work began. At the same time the report by an external consultant commissioned by the Department to examine the proposed development found that its plans were over-ambitious and of doubtful feasibility given the unstable and uncertain circumstance surrounding the development. The consultant's report included the following recommendations:

- That systems development should be restricted to functional areas essential to support initial TEC operations (this was to be acted upon by the Department)
- That the new system should be piloted in a small number of TECs before placing the software on general release (this was not acted upon).

The consultant's August 1989 report also found that some of the personnel assigned to the project lacked experience essential to the management of a project of this scale, and that the risks of relying on untried managers were unacceptable. It recommended that these posts be filled by experienced personnel, or at the very least, be supported by such individuals. Due to a shortage of suitable staff within the Department this recommendation was not acted upon. At the time TFS was planned there was no Information Systems Strategy within the Department of Employment.

The Field System was a large and complex integrated system that was to run on a series of distributed minicomputers. The development proceeded without any involvement from the TECs during the design phase of the new system. It was only in April 1991, around eighteen months into the development process, that the TECs (following encouragement from the Department) formed a national user group to represent their views on the system. By this time, however, some TECs had been operating for a year and with the bulk of the system having already been released (although many changes were still to be made).

The specification of TFS had been laid down, by necessity, without the involvement of the TECs who were to use it. When the information needs of the Department and the TECs became more clearly defined it became necessary to make significant changes to the system design. This was to place additional pressure on the software development teams who were already working to a tight deadline. This pressure was to be increased when, following the release of version 1 of the software, resources were allocated to deal with the large number of change requests made and correct the errors reported (in total, almost 7000 errors and change requests were to be logged). This had the effect of diverting resources from the development as a whole. The situation was exacerbated by the fact that an effective system to control and prioritize system changes was implemented only in December 1991—around two years after the project had begun.

The testing of the early versions of the system was ineffective, with software being released to the TECs still containing a large number of errors. This was due not only to problems with the software and its documentation but also to the slippage in the project schedule reducing the time available for testing.

It was originally planned that the hardware and the ten software sub-systems (to be rolled out in four phases) that make up The Field System would be implemented as follows:

Stage	Date
Delivery of hardware	January–September 1990
Implementation of first phase	January 1990
Implementation of fourth phase	September 1991
Post-implementation review	October 1991

However, the problems associated with the design, development and testing of the initial software led to this plan being abandoned and software modules being released as they became available. By November 1992 the TECs had received 17 versions of the software, with each version being a combination of fixes to existing modules and releases of additional functions. The 21 TECs that became operational before the core software (accounting modules) had been completed were provided with manual systems prior to moving to the early releases of TFS.

The support offered to the TECs was considered by an external review in April 1991 to be poor. It was reported that the training manuals and System Guides were difficult to use and the helpdesk was staffed by casual workers who did not possess much knowledge of the system. This meant that many queries were passed on to the development team, with the result that not only was there a slow response to queries but also that development work was disrupted, further impeding the project's progress. These problems were to be recognized with the helpdesk being staffed by more experienced people and user manuals improved.

The post-implementation review, originally scheduled for October 1991, had not been carried out at the time of the NAO study (August 1992). It was the intention of the Department to make out a full review in September 1993.[13]

The Field System had been promoted to the TECs as a user-friendly management information system. However, most TECs did not agree and found TFS to be slow, cumbersome to use and far from user-friendly. Of the 71 (out of a total of 75) TECs that replied to a NAO questionnaire, none were using all the facilities provided by TFS, with many employing only a few of the sub-systems available. And although six TECs were not using TFS at all, having preferred to purchase their own systems, most used the core payments and accounting components of the system.

An external review of TEC information systems carried out in September 1992 found that it was likely that the TECs would move away from using TFS. This result was confirmed by a NAO survey which also found that of the 65 TECs that were making some use of TFS facilities, 29 intended to either reduce their reliance on the system or else replace it within the year.

In September 1992 the Department of Employment announced that it would withdraw from The Field System and pass responsibility for information technology, that is, the support and future development of TFS, to the TECs themselves. The Field System's hardware and software would be given to the TECs to enable them to continue to use and develop the system if desired. It was the view of the NAO that this decision was a direct result of the problems with TFS experienced by the Department since it was not underpinned by any detailed analysis of the TEC's situation.

Of the many conclusions contained in the NAO report the following section is very relevant to the contents of this chapter:

> ...in its earlier stages, The Field System exemplified many of the deficiencies commonly found in recent years in the management and control of government computer projects. ... The System has further demonstrated that:

---

[13] This date was selected as it would mark the final transfer of responsibility for TFS to the TECs.

- projects need to be subject to rigorous and realistic risk assessment, not least when requirements and timescales change, so that they proceed on the basis of well informed strategic decisions by senior management;
- the best possible user involvement from the outset is important to help to ensure that the project meets its intended purpose; and
- effective project management is vital to success especially where the project is particularly challenging.

Veterans Benefits Administration—A Failure Avoided?[14]

This case examines how a timely review by the US General Accounting Office of plans to modernize information systems within the Veterans Benefits Administration (VBA) probably saved it from becoming yet another IS failure.

The VBA is part of the US Department of Veteran Affairs (VA) and is concerned with the distribution of non-medical benefits to nearly 27 million veterans and their dependants. The largest area administered by the VBA (a major Division of Department of Veterans Affairs), accounting for over 96% of benefit payments, is compensation and pensions (C&P). In 1991 the VBA handled over 3.5 million new or existing C&P claims worth over $16 billion (£10.3 billion).

At the end of the 1980s the VBA's existing centralized mainframe computer systems were each based around specific benefit programmes and the information held could not easily be integrated to support all the VBA's programmes. In 1990 the Secretary of Veteran Affairs requested that the VBA make fundamental changes in its provision of services to veterans, making special reference to the need to change its business processes, procedures and use of technology. In response the centrepiece of the VBA's modernization plan was the replacement of its existing systems with a decentralized system that integrates all information held about a veteran (then held on several different systems) into a single master record. This would enable claims to be processed more

---
....

[14] The details in this case come from GAO (1992b).

quickly. It was also hoped to improve the service offered by the VBA through the use of document imaging, workflow systems and expert systems.

Since the 1980 Paperwork Reduction Act the Department of Veterans Affairs has had a senior official with the responsibility to act as the focal point for all its information management activities. This role (Chief Information Resource Officer—CIRO) was enhanced in 1991 when, following a reorganization, the CIRO was given authority to manage information resources across the Department as a whole.

In order to achieve its modernization objectives the VBA developed the following three-stage procurement plan:

- *Stage I* Acquire hardware and software (including host computers, operating systems, database management systems, workstations, workflow systems, software development tools)
- *Stage II* Acquire and install imaging systems (within regional offices), and storage sub-systems (at each of the ten processing sites)
- *Stage III* Replacement of mainframe computers (specific requirements yet to be determined)

It was planned that the design and development of the new applications would run in parallel to the acquisition of the new hardware and software. The new applications would be designed to replicate the functions of the existing systems in addition to supporting (the as-yet undefined) new business processes. The VBA's Information Resources Management (IRM) Office was to lead the modernization effort and be responsible for the design and coding of all applications software.

It was expected that the whole programme would be completed by 1998 at a cost of $256 million, the purchase of hardware and software accounting for $94 million of this amount.

The General Accounting Office (GAO) review of the VBA modernization effort revealed that their plans were flawed in a number of respects.

Technology-led Modernization Strategy

It was the intention of the VBA to purchase the hardware and software for the new system before they had defined their future information needs. The VBA's IRM Office had done little work towards defining its new information architecture.[15] The contents of the new veteran master record, intended to be the centrepiece of the new system, had not been defined. The VBA had also failed to define the information requirements of the benefits programmes it administers, and had not examined how they would relate to the veteran master record.

This technology-led approach ignored the GSA (General Services Administration) guidelines governing the development and design of information systems. These guidelines advise that a structured, systematic approach towards the definition of future information needs must be adopted before proceeding to purchase the hardware and software required.

Current Business Processes Poorly Understood

The major part of the work of the VBA is processing claims related to C&P, with the average claim taking 151 days to process. This was acknowledged to be unacceptable and was to be reduced by the elimination of delays within the process. There was, however, disagreement over the cause of the delays.

The C&P management attributed the reason for the length of this process to delays by staff in the regional offices who fail promptly to request and receive the information they need to process a claim. This was in contrast to VBA's IRM Office modernization studies, that indicated that the delays were caused by problems associated with the existing paper-based system, with documents being hard to locate, misfiled, or lost and being difficult to retrieve from central storage facilities. The solution to these delays proposed by the modernization studies was to use an imaging system linked to workflow software to enable claims to be automatically routed through the claims process.

The GAO conducted their own investigation into the C&P claims process and discovered that the neither C&P management not the VBA's IRM Office fully understood the process. The GAO discovered that in dealing with a C&P claim the 151 days broke down as follows:

---------........

[15] An information architecture is a model that shows the major processes of a system, the data used by those processes, and the relationships between them.

Days

63	waiting for information (from VHA, the military services, the veteran, etc.)
4	transfer files between staff
0.21	working on a claim (5 hours)
83	waiting for someone to work on the claim
Total 151	(approx.)

The imaging/workflow solution proposed by the VBA was analysed by the GAO in the light of the above information. It was found that since 55% of the time to process a claim was taken up in waiting for someone to work on the claim, the proposal would have the potential to reduce the time taken to process a claim by only 6–12 days. In the light of this information it was recognized that the modernization plans could result in only marginal improvements in the level of service offered by the VBA.

It was also discovered that the legal status of the electronic documents to be held within the proposed imaging system was unclear. In May 1991 the Department's General Council had raised a number of concerns, including whether the Court of Veterans Appeals would accept electronic records as evidence. These issues had not been resolved before the modernization plan was formulated.

Goals of System Unclear

The modernization effort of the VBA was not based on the achievement of any defined outcomes. The VBA had not outlined any specific levels of service to be achieved nor had performance indicators, to measure progress towards achievement of service levels, been established. The VBA also did not intend to use a formal review process to examine whether the new system actually had improved the level of service offered to veterans. The justification for this approach was that there were too many factors, including changes in legislation, that make measuring the contribution of the new system too difficult.

Poor Communication

The GAO found that there was a lack of effective communication and a poor working relationship between those responsible for creating the new system (the IRM Office) and the C&P managers who were to use it. This situation had worsened due to the failure of the IRM Office to encourage user participation in the decision-making process surrounding the modernization.

Managers within the C&P programme offices had been unable to see how the new system would address their business problems and believed that the IRM Office were acquiring information technology solutions without any regard for their needs. IRM officials, on the other hand, believed that C&P managers found it difficult to think creatively to solve problems and revise their work processes, and that the introduction of new technology would force them to change their ways of working.

CIRO Lacked Jurisdiction over VBA

The problems within the VBA modernization process highlighted the fact that, despite the 1991 reorganization, the Department of Veterans Affairs CIRO still lacked the authority to intervene in the decisions being made within the VBA. The involvement of the CIRO had been limited to reviewing the procurement process of the VBA modernization effort.

The limitations of the VBA strategy was recognized by the CIRO but the management of the Department of Veterans Affairs had little influence over events, primarily as a result of the budget structure that permits the VBA to control its own financial resources.

The recommendations of the GAO report to the Secretary of Veteran Affairs were as folows:

- Postpone contract award for any procurement under the modernization scheme until VBA
  i analyses its current business processes and develops a clear understanding of the deficiencies and problems the effort is intended to resolve;
  ii identifies specific goals for improved service and develops a formal process to ensure that the modernized system meets those goals;
  iii completely defines its new information architecture;
  iv ensures effective participation and communication between senior (C&P) program and IRM managers
- Ensure that the CIRO has authority for defining, designing, and implementing the modernization effort. This should include authority

and responsibility for leading the analysis of the current benefits delivery processes, establishing service delivery goals, and developing plans for how information technology should be used to provide better service to veterans.

Lessons from Government Computer Projects

The events described in both the detailed and the smaller cases above represent a small part of what has become a huge volume of government information systems activity. The catalogue of management failures recorded in this chapter can be seen as a microcosm of the challenges that all managers must face in making effective use of information technology within their organizations. Many of the events described above could equally have occurred within commercial organizations faced with the same problems. Their occurrence within government systems developments has simply had the dual effect of magnifying the consequences and laying them open to public view. The lessons outlined below should thus be viewed as being of general applicability to the conduct of information systems developments in both the commercial and government sectors.

Organizational Lessons

Coherent strategic planning

In two of the three major cases discussed above, Wessex and the VBA, there was a strategic vision that was not translated into detailed strategic planning. In the other case, TFS, there is little evidence to suggest that there was either any strategic vision or any coherent strategic planning.

It is just as pointless possessing a strategic vision that cannot be realized as it is to try to realize a system that has no strategic context. The fact that the Wessex case fell into the former and the VBA and TFS cases into the latter, of these categories would have dramatically increased the risk they would fail.

A coherent strategic vision, fully informed by a detailed understanding of the future needs of the organization, is an essential starting point for strategic planning, which in turn provides a basis for the realization of the vision.

The role of leadership

Positive consistent leadership plays an important part in the definition and realization of an information systems strategy. However, very strong leadership can be detrimental, since it can stifle the healthy debate necessary to obtain the grass–roots feedback essential to the success of any development. The danger is that although the strategy and its weaknesses are well known among those working on the development, it becomes impossible to pass this information to those at the very top.

The frequent leadership changes that occurred within the Social Security Administration and the many changes made to strategy produced precisely the opposite result, with the organization lacking confidence that any strategy will endure. Once lost in this manner, organizational confidence is very hard to rebuild.

Organizational oversight

Structures should be in place to provide an informed oversight of the progress of systems developments. Informed structures allow individuals or groups that have the responsibility and the experience to estimate accurately the true state of an information systems development. The Veterans and Wessex cases both provide examples in which those responsible for the oversight of the development did not have sufficient expertise to make an accurate assessment of the status of the project.

Project Lessons

Technology-led solutions

The dangers of adopting a technology-led solution to an organizational problem are illustrated within the Wessex, Veterans and Field System cases. In focusing on the technology required to solve a perceived problem rather than encouraging user participation first to define the problem and then assist in developing an appropriate solution, these organizations were adopting a strategy that almost guaranteed failure.

Technology-led solutions are proposed by those who understand (or think they understand) both the technology and the problem. It is far more likely however, that those who propose such a solution do not understand either the technology or the problem. This is due to two main reasons. First, technology-led solutions will tend to propose the use of leading-edge technologies in which no-one (not even the supplier) may fully understand the full implications of their application to a particular set of problems. To propose their use in (usually ambitious) settings is thus more an act of faith than a suggestion based on practical experience. The second reason is that pure technology-led solutions tend to exist in the absence of any detailed appreciation of organizational and user requirements, since the pure world of technology is inevitably debased by knowledge of how messy the real world actually is. Technology-led solutions are really saying 'this is how the world ought to be', and are thus flawed.

Continuity of management

Changes of management at the project level act to undermine the accountability of individuals. As managers anticipate a move they can defer difficult decisions or adopt risky solutions in the knowledge that they will not be around when the chickens come home to roost. It is thus difficult to maintain a strong line of accountability, since the manager who has moved on is able to defend the original decision and blame its implementation, whereas the manager currently in post can blame the original decision as the source of the problem.

VARIATIONS ON A THEME

It is sad, but probably true, that it would be possible to fill an entire book with cases of non-military government software engineering disasters. This is probably not because government employees are any more, or less, incompetent or unlucky than anyone else, rather that the level of public accountability is much higher than in commercial organizations. Having said this, here are a few more cases of flawed government projects.

FmHA—It's Hard to Get There If You Aren't Sure Where You're Going...

The Farmers Home Administration or FmHA has not been very successful in its attempts to use technology to support its operations. In

1991 the GAO found that the FmHA's attempt to modernize its systems to administer its loan programme, representing its third attempt to reach the same goal since the mid-1970s, was once again poorly thought out (GAO, 1991b). The $520 million (£347 million) new technology programme did not link into a strategic business plan that provided a view of how the Agency would operate. Worse still, the new technology plan did not even take account of the structural and operational changes currently under way within the FmHA. The GAO expressed serious doubt over the ability of the FmHA to make effective use of technology to improve its operations.

IRS—If at First You Don't Succeed... (GAO, 1992c)

Much of the IRS tax processing system dates from the 1960s, and uses data processing methods like batch processing with magnetic tapes that go back even further. It has long been recognized that the system should be updated and the fact that it hasn't been is not for want of trying.

The first major modernization effort undertaken by the IRS commenced in 1968 with a redesign of the entire system to take advantage of (what was then) more advanced technology. This was abandoned in 1978 due to congressional concerns about the security of the proposed system and the cost of the whole programme. In 1982 the second programme was initiated with the IRS examining three separate approaches to modernization over the four years to 1986. None of these approaches got any further than the planning stage due to repeated changes of leadership, a lack of clear management responsibility for the programme, and the lack of technical and managerial expertise within the IRS itself.

In 1986 the IRS begun its current (third) modernization programme. This programme, known as Tax Systems Modernisation (TSM) is expected to cost tens of billions of dollars and will not be completed until well into the next century.[16] Let's hope it'll be third time lucky for the IRS.

-----------········

[16] A recent estimate (1993) anticipated that TSM would be fully implemented by 2008 at a cost of $23 billion (£15.3 billion).

Foreign Office Fiasco[17]

The UK Foreign Office (FO) were left with egg on their face when government auditors were unable to make sense of their 1990 accounts due to a breakdown in their computer systems. The auditor could not verify the spending claims made by the FO because all the evidence was trapped inside the malfunctioning computer.

The decision to upgrade the FO computer systems was just the start of their problems. The cost of the redevelopment was initially put at £560 000 ($840 000), but by the completion of the project this figure had risen to £937,000 ($1.4 million). Worse still, the software house that had undertook the work went into liquidation just after the system was finally installed.

The changeover to the new systems was not properly handled and before it could be completed a hard disk shattered in the old system, the information it held being lost as a result. The FO moved over to the new system which it then began to realize was not working properly either, posting money to wrong accounts and shutting down for no apparent reason. A high turnover in book-keeping staff also led to further errors being made.

In order to try to sort out the mess the FO employed someone from their failed software supplier on a £53 000 per annum consultancy contract.

References

Committee of Public Accounts, *Foreign and Commonwealth Office: Qualification of accounts 1989–90*, HMSO, July (1991).

Committee of Public Accounts, *Wessex Regional Health Authority Regional Information Systems Plan*, HMSO, November (1993).

Committee of Public Accounts, *The Department of Employment: The Field System*, HMSO, January (1994).

GAO, *SSA Computers: Long-Range Vision Needed to Guide Future Systems Modernisation*, GAO/IMTEC-91-44, September (1991a).

GAO, *ADP Modernization: Half-Billion Dollar FmHA Effort Lacks Adequate Planning and Oversight*, GAO/IMTEC-92-9, October (1991b).

---

[17] Based on Committee of Public Accounts (1991) and *Guardian Weekly* (1991).

GAO, *Information Resources: Summary of Federal Agencies' Information Resources Management Problems*, GAO/IMTEC-92-13FS, February (1992a).

GAO, *Veterans Benefits—Acquisitions of Information Resources for Modernisation is Premature*, GAO/IMTEC-93-6, November (1992b).

GAO, *Internal Revenue Service Issues*, GAO/OCG-93-24TR, December (1992c).

GAO, *Executive Guide: Improving Mission Performance Through Strategic Information Management and Technology*, May (1994).

Guardian Weekly, 'High-tech blackout', 17 February (1991).

National Audit Office, *Managing Computer Projects in the National Health Service*, HMSO, November (1990).

National Audit Office, *Computer Systems for Training and Enterprise Councils: The Department of Employment's Management of The Field System*, HMSO, June (1993).

7

CONCLUSIONS
WHAT CAN BE LEARNED?

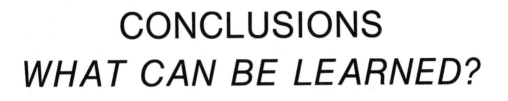

When you're failing, you're forced to be creative, to dig deep and
think hard, night and day.
Every company needs people who have been through that. Every
company needs people who have made mistakes and then made the
most of them.[1]

Where there is much desire to learn, there of necessity will be much
arguing, much writing, many opinions; for opinion in good men is
but knowledge in the making.[2]

[1] Bill Gates, *The Guardian*, 27 April 1995.
[2] John Milton, *Areopagitica*, 1644.

To try to learn something from the failed systems we have looked at so far an attempt will be made to distil from the complex events within each of the cases examined the factors that played a part in the failure. These factors will form the basis for the identification of a set of generic failure factors, called Critical Failure Factors (CFFs), that may be useful in providing a set of cautionary pointers to those involved in the conduct of IS developments. But it has long been recognized that there are, alas, no easy answers in this area and it is likely that IS developments will remain the untamed beasts they have always been—apparently docile, but able to turn nasty at any moment. Fred Brooks (1987) made this point perfectly when he wrote:

> Of all the monsters that fill the nightmares of our folklore, none terrify more than the werewolves, because they transform unexpectedly from the familiar into horrors. For these, one seeks bullets of silver that can magically lay them to rest.
> The familiar software project, at least as seen by the nontechnical manager, has something of this character; it is usually innocent and straightforward, but is capable of becoming a monster of missed schedules, blown budgets, and flawed products.

This observation, written in the second half of the 1980s, is probably as true now as it was then. But we should not, we cannot, throw up our hands in despair and say 'there is nothing to be done' about managing complex IS developments. Neither should we believe that the many magic 'solutions'—from methodologies to object orientation—provide an easy answer to the problem of building large complex software systems. Perhaps the best, and most realistic, solution is to recognize that there will be no magic fix for the problems of managing complex IS developments and rather content ourselves with incremental improvements to all parts of the process. This chapter will introduce a simple approach, based around a series of CFFs, that is designed to help managers quickly to identify troubled projects and enable them to take appropriate remedial action. This approach is intended to be of use by all technical and non-technical managers involved in an IS development and it is designed to enable managers to stand back and assess the true status of a project. It is hoped that the CFF framework will thus provide a means of obtaining a 'reality check' on a project and serve as an incremental improvement to the whole business of building complex information systems.

Introducing the Critical Failure Factor

Information Systems projects of any size are highly complex combinations of organizational, financial, technical, human, and political factors. The success or failure of a project will very likely occur as a result of the obvious and subtle interactions between these factors. What emerges from the case studies in the preceding chapters of this book are the factors that are associated with an IS development becoming either a failure or a disaster. Such factors, CFFs, are the crucial elements of a project that, when they are in a less than optimal state, will increase the chance that an IS project will either fail or at worst, become a disaster.

The view of IS developments outlined in Figure 7.1, that IS projects and their management are encapsulated within an organizational context, will be used to explore the CFFs that have been identified. What emerges is a series of factors that served either to foster the development of systems that were likely to become failures or prolong the pre-termination period in which resources continued to be allocated to what had become a lost cause. In some cases this termination period was so protracted that IS failures were turned into full-scale IS disasters. The CFFs are shown in Figure 7.2.

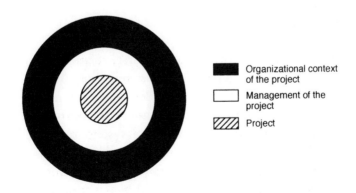

Figure 7.1 IS developments

Organizational context
Hostile culture
Poor reporting structures

Management of project
Over-commitment
Political pressures

Conduct of the project
Initiation phase
  Technology focused
  Lure of leading edge
  Complexity underestimated

Analysis & Design phase
  Poor consultation
  Design by committee
  Technical 'fix' for management problem
  Poor procurement

Development phase
  Staff turnover
  Competency
  Communication

Implementation phase
  Receding deadlines
  Inadequate testing
  Inadequate user training

Figure 7.2 Critical Failure Factors

The terms failure and disaster are, of course, relative. Even though the cost of the LAS despatch system was a relatively low £1.5 million ($2.25 million), the implications for the people of London of its collapse mean that it must be classed as an IS disaster. In comparison, the failure of the Confirm hotel/car-rental reservation system may well have been extremely costly for the organizations involved (with AMR alone writing off some $213 million on the failed project), but may be classed as a failure (albeit a major failure) since it was probably not central to any of the organizations involved. The Taurus project at the London

Stock Exchange, on the other hand, is almost certainl$_\cdot$
organization since it probably not only served to we$_\cdot$
Stock Exchange within the City of London but also
long-term future. An IS failure thus has an impac$_\cdot$
or organizational level, whereas an IS disaster w$_\cdot$
broader base such as customers or the general pub$_\cdot$
strategic implications for the organization involved.

The CFFs discussed below are a set of generic factors that are app$_\cdot$
able to any development project. They are intended to provide a means
of identifying at an early stage the combinations of circumstances in
which IS developments may move from potential success to potential
failure, or from failure to disaster. The presence of any one CFF may, in
itself, not be sufficient to push a project into failure. However, the larger
the number of CFFs that are identified, the greater are the chances that a
development will result in an IS failure, a major IS failure, or an IS
disaster.

Critical Failure Factors—The Organizational Context of the Project

Hostile Culture

One of the major foundations for IS project success or failure is the culture
that exists at organizational/project level. In some cultures it is of positive
individual benefit *not* to be the bringer of bad news for, as history demonstrates, those in charge may find it hard to resist shooting the messenger.
Perhaps worst of all, as a 'reward' the messenger may be given the task of
finding solutions for the problems that have been identified.

So, within such a culture there can easily be a dislocation of the
reporting structure surrounding the project with the effect that bad
news may either be moderated or fail to be passed on. Such an information dislocation will almost inevitably leave senior staff with an incomplete picture of what is going on.

A further feature of such fear-based cultures may be the tendency to
'scapegoat' those who may be identified with failure. This tendency
increases the chances that managers dealing with a troubled project will
'press on' rather than call for an early review, with possibly disastrous
consequences.

oor Reporting Structures

One factor that runs as a common theme through many of the cases in this book is the fact that senior management were apparently not aware of what was going on in the major IS developments for which they were ultimately responsible. Although they were obviously interested, they were not truly involved. They were not 'In the bubble'.[3]

It is perhaps understandable why senior management would allow themselves to become disconnected from the major development projects under their control. IS projects are often protracted affairs that take months or years to complete, involving masses of complex technical detail and jargon that may be unfamiliar to many Board members. Few senior managers may have the expertise, interest, or time to take special interest in the progress of an individual project and may prefer instead to rely upon the technical staff to produce the goods as promised. Once this situation has occurred, senior managers are no longer 'in the bubble' and have effectively abdicated their responsibility in favour of the project managers. Their major source of information about the progress of the project is now that same project management who have so much to lose if the project starts to falter. This is not a situation that is guaranteed to provide an unbiased reporting of a project's progress. Commenting on the problems that complexity brings to the development of large-scale systems Fernando Corbato (1991) has written:

> The most obvious complexity problems arise from scale. In particular, the larger the personnel required, the more levels of management there will be. . . . The difficulty is that with more layers of management, the top-most layers become out of touch with the relevant bottom issues and the likelihood of random serendipitous communication decreases.
>
> Another problem of organizations is that subordinates hate to report bad news, sometimes for fear of 'being shot as the messenger' and at other times because they may have a different set of goals than the upper management.
>
> And finally, large projects encourge specialization so that few team

---

[3] I am indebted to Gene Rochlin of the University of California at Berkeley for introducing me to this concept. A more detailed discussion may be found in La Porte (1991).

members understand all of the project. Misunderstandings and miscommunication begin, and soon a significant part of the project resources are spent fighting internal confusion. And, of course, mistakes occur.

Perhaps the main alternative open to senior management to discover the state of a doubtful project may simply be a project review. However, a project review is not without problems since it is likely to be disruptive, time-consuming and may have a negative effect upon project morale. In fact, a study by the GSA on large-scale government IS developments found that, of all the problems that may arise, audits by the GAO during the planning and procurement phases ranked sixth! (GAO, 1988).

The instigation of such a review may also be interpreted as a vote of no confidence in both the project and its management. As a result such a review is likely to be resisted by both the project's supporters on the Board and the project management team. Despite the drawbacks to project reviews there are very few avenues open to Board members that provide the impartial information the board must have. It is perhaps worth recalling that had an early project review been instigated for the PROMS project at the Performing Right Society it would have cost less than £200 000 ($300 000) and uncovered the errors that were to lead to the loss of 2 years' work and the waste of some £8 million ($12 million)[4]. However, it also worth recalling that the decision to proceed with the development in the first place was itself taken after a review had validated the project design.

A truly impartial project review on its own is not enough, however, since the findings must also be used as the basis for further action. Having lost the battle to prevent a review, it is likely that a project's supporters would seek to undermine and discredit its findings, thereby protecting the project from further interference. The experience of the Confirm project may be appropriate in this context.

A key element affecting the way in which the information contained in routine progress reports and project reviews will be viewed is the

---

[4] These figures are taken from the *PRS Summary of PROMS Assessment*, p. 3.

importance of the project to the organization as a whole. Developments that are central to the purpose of the organization may become a 'sacred cow' and be closely identified with the organization itself. Once a project is elevated to this status speaking out against it becomes tantamount to open disloyalty to the organization itself and, whatever the truth of the statements, will be strongly discouraged. An atmosphere is thus created in which the project will be viewed more positively than the reports of its progress would justify. This analysis could well have been the case in the majority of the projects examined within this book.

An external project review may, however, provide that fresh view that results in the spell being broken. From being an organizational 'sacred cow' a project can very rapidly become the technological equivalent of the emperor's new clothes, with all involved suddenly seeing the project as it really is. In this situation it is often instructive to observe the realignment of a projects erstwhile supporters, proving the truth in the old saying that 'success has many parents, but failure is an orphan'.

A simpler and cheaper alternative to project review, and perhaps the most cost-effective method of ensuring managers are kept in touch with the problems and issues concerning those working on the front line of a development, is the use of an anonymous suggestion box.

Critical Failure Factors—Management of the Project

Over-commitment[5]

One of the factors that is central to the eventual success of an IS development is the commitment of the management group responsible for the project. However, the constant danger is that such commitment may develop, in time, into a state of over-commitment to the eventual success of the project. Over-commitment to a project is perhaps one of the most important reasons preventing the early cancellation of failed IS developments and is probably responsible for many IS development failures being prolonged until they become IS disasters.

_____ ....

[5] A more detailed discussion of the psychology of overcommitment to particular course of action may be found in Staw and Ross (1987a).

Over-commitment to a course of action develops over time due to the subtle interaction of a number of social and psychological factors and results in managers being unable to take an impartial view of the project as a whole. Once this happens a manager becomes 'too close' to a project and can no longer maintain the impartiality necessary to operate efficiently. One of the most obvious effects of over-commitment is the, usually unconscious, tendency to regard all information about the project from a biased standpoint. Reports will be mentally sifted and information favourable to the project extracted and used to justify continued work, while adverse information will be ignored or undermined. This in turn can give rise to progress reports to senior managers giving a far more optimistic picture than would otherwise be the case.

Another facet of being 'too close' to a project is the situation in which a manager's success or failure can become closely identified with the success or failure of a particular development. In this situation, if a project gets into trouble, there will be a tendency for the manager to choose to allocate more resources in the hope that the situation can be retrieved rather than conduct a full reassessment of the project's current chances of success. Few people like to admit past errors and it is a natural, if sometimes misguided, reaction to problems to persist with a chosen course of action in the hope that you will be proved right in the end. The social pressures that often exist within organizations will often mean that this need to avoid failure and prove that you were justified in the original course of action will only be heightened. An extreme case of this was perhaps exhibited by Howard Hughes in his decision to build the giant wooden sea-plane that later came to be known as the Spruce Goose. While few thought it would ever fly (and apart from a single test-flight it never did), Hughes became committed to building it rather than admit it had been a mistake.

A further aspect of over-commitment are the factors that encourage managers to persevere with a troubled project despite mounting difficulties. Such perseverance can sometimes arise from successes that may have been achieved in the past despite difficult circumstances, leading to the observation that past successes are not necessarily the best training for dealing with current failures. Another factor that encourages perseverance is related to the culture of the organization in which it is expected that managers will 'stick with it' when the going gets tough. If such tenacity is indeed a valued part of being a manager failing projects will probably not be caught early before too much damage has been caused. It will be far more likely that projects will be cancelled later rather than sooner, with all that this implies.

It is very likely that over-commitment was a significant factor in prolonging the demise of projects that have been examined within this book. The cases in which it is perhaps most graphically displayed are those involving the London Ambulance Service, the London Stock Exchange and the Performing Right Society.

The tendency to get locked into an escalating course of action that seems doomed to failure is often easier to recognize in people other than yourself. However, although the tendency to over-commit to a project in which we have invested much personal capital cannot be denied, it can be recognized and avoided. The first step to dealing with over-commitment is its recognition, and Figure 7.3 illustrates a series of questions that, if answered honestly, may provide the basis for developing such a recognition.

Once over-commitment has been recognized there are a number of strategies that may be used to reduce its effects and avoid its recurrence. The following shortlist is an indication of some of the most common methods:

- *Establishing an 'open' project culture* One way of keeping in touch with project realities is to create an environment in which concerns and issues can be discussed openly within a project without fear of any repercussions. An 'open-door' policy among project management and weekly project meetings in which critical evaluation within the group is encouraged and the role of devils advocate is played, perhaps in rotation, by one or more members of the group.
- *Separation of project management and project reporting functions* The separation of the role of project manager from the role of reporting project progress and updating the overall project plan can provide the basis for more impartiality within the formal reporting process. While in itself no guarantee of unbiased reporting to senior management, such division should reduce the possibility of partial reports being used to justify further work.
- *Impartial reviews of progress* The imposition, actual or threatened, of

How, then, can managers know whether they have crossed the threshold between the determination to get things done and over-commitment? Although the distinction is often subtle, they can clarify matters by asking themselves the following questions:

1 Do I have trouble defining what would constitute failure for this project or decision? Is my definition of failure ambiguous, or does it shift as the project evolves?
2 Would failure on this project radically change the way I think of myself as a manager or as a person? Have I bet the ranch on this venture for my career or for my own satisfaction?
3 Do I have trouble hearing other people's concerns about the project, and do I sometimes evaluate others' competence on the basis of their support for the project?
4 Do I generally evaluate how various events and actions will affect the project before I think about how they'll affect other areas of the organization or the company as a whole?
5 Do I sometimes feel that if this project ends, there will be no tomorrow?

If a manager has answered yes to one or more of these questions, the person is probably over-commited to a project.

Reproduced with permission from Staw and Ross (1987a).

Figure 7.3 See escalation for what it is

periodic reviews on progress is likely to be a very sobering thought for those working on a project. Although this is a very powerful weapon in the fight against over-commitment it should be used with some care since it can be both disruptive and demotivating to the entire project team. It may also be prudent to allow time for reviews within the original project plan.

- *Reassigning managers* The simplest, if sometimes rather brutal, method of curing perceived over-commitment is to reassign and replace one or more of a project's management team. The new regime is likely to carry none of the baggage of past decisions and can take a clean-sheet approach to the project. However, since a change in project management will inevitably undermine management continuity it should be viewed very much as a last resort.

Decision-making Escalation—Throwing Good Money After Bad

The many factors outlined above that may result in managers becoming over-committed to a course of action forms part of the larger area of debate surrounding decision-making escalation. Once a development has reached a certain stage the weight of previous decisions may mean that managers and organizations become 'locked' into continuing with a failing project. While such behaviour may be a phenomenon we can all recognize, understanding exactly why decision-making escalation occurs is the subject of much research. One useful approach[6] to this problem proposes a four-stage escalation model in which different sets of factors act to foster escalation at different stages of a project (Table 7.1).

Stage 1—Project Factors

The focus at the start of a project, and its reason for approval, is on the benefits that will flow if it is successful. However, once the project is underway (and possibly in difficulty) interest in the benefits and costs of a system may shift to concentrate on other areas. The costs associated with cancellation will now become important, with factors such as reluctance to write off the investment already made on a project, its negligible scrap value and potentially high close-down costs may all act against project cancellation and foster escalation. Indeed, it may be that the pressure acting against closure is likely to be increased if the hoped-for benefits of a successful project are large.

Table 7.1 Four stage escalation model

Stage	Escalation factors	Project abandonment occurs
1	Project	—
2	Psychological	—
3	Social	PRS, Confirm
4	Structural	LAS, Taurus

───────····⋯⋯

[6] See Staw and Ross (1987). Another article that examines escalation in an organisational context is Drummond (1994).

Stage 2—Psychological Factors

As the first difficulties arise a range of psychological factors are thought to take over as the engine of escalation. The psychological need for those involved in the project to have their earlier decisions proved right may result in the biasing of information, as outlined above. This may in turn lead on to the scale of the problems with a project being under-stated by those involved with the perceived risks of a project being underestimated, enabling escalating decisions to be made against a background of apparently low risk.

Stage 3—Social Factors

As it becomes harder to avoid the reality of the situation it is thought that a range of factors concerning the social context of those involved in the project now become the most important contributor to decision-making escalation. Such factors include the situation in which indivi-duals, and their future prospects, become personally identified with the success or failure of a project. In addition, factors such as job insecurity, the existence of a competitive work environment, the imitation of how other (apparently successful) managers would react in similar situations, and organizational expectations may also be important. Finally, the simple desire to save face may also act as an important factor in encoura-ging decision-making escalation.

Stage 4—Structural Factors

As the project continues and the social factors promoting escalation become diluted as the number of individuals involved in the project grows, so-called structural factors are thought to take over as the primary agents of escalation. Structural factors are the result of the hardening of organizational commitment to a project and may include corporate pride, the existence of internal political pressures resisting cancellation and promoting continuance, the administrative inertia inherent in any bureaucracy, and the fact that key managers may have become entrenched in their support for a project.

If we attempt to locate the major cases within this four-stage escalation model, then it can be seen that the challenge for organizations is to identify potential escalation problems as soon as possible, and certainly to prevent escalation moving to the structural stage. It might be argued that

cases explored earlier managed to prevent escalation
il it reached stage 4, with structural factors becoming
r its continuance. The challenge for organizations is
ns in which potential project failures can be identi-
stage in their lifecycle and decision-making escala-

...ssures

Organizations are not machines, even though some of those
running them would dearly like them to be so. They are
communities of people, and therefore behave just like other
communities. They compete amongst themselves for power and
resources, there are differences of opinion and of values, conflicts of
priorities and of goals. There are those who want to change things
and those who would willingly settle for a quiet life. There are
pressure groups and lobbies, cliques and cabals, rivalries and
contests, clashes of personality and bonds of alliance.
It would be odd if it were not so, and foolish of anyone to pretend
that in some ideal world those differences would not exist
(Handy, 1993).

An important part of virtually any IS development is the political
dimension of the project. Whether it is recognized or not by those
involved in the development, the politics surrounding a project can have
an important affect upon its progress and even its eventual success or
failure.[8] The political dimension of a project is multi-faceted and
although there is not space enough to explore the subject fully here the
major case studies illustrate several of the most important dangers of this
aspect of the IS development process.

Influential Outsiders

A potential problem for any project is the presence of powerful outsiders
who are able to exert an influence on the progress of the development.

....

[7] An interesting and readable discussion of research surrounding de-escalation may be found in
Drummond (1995).
[8] A wider discussion of this topic may be found in Block (1983).

These outsiders may be interested, although not directly involved, in the everyday management of the project and will generally have some political interest themselves in its success or failure. The project may, however, be just a single pawn in what is a larger political chess game and, if it is lost or sacrificed, may not unduly affect their overall position. Indeed, their relationship to the project will almost certainly be structured so that the payoff from success will be maximized but the fallout from failure minimized.

This relationship between powerful outsiders and the project is perhaps typified by the setting of an early date when the system will go live. This one action, if the project meets the date and is successful, will tend to maximise the payoff to the powerful outsider—say the project sponsor—but is likely to increase the problems faced by the project management team itself. This problem may be one of the most common forms of outside interference in a project, and also one which carries some of the greatest risks.

The London Ambulance Service case study, although perhaps an extreme case, illustrates perfectly the dangers of interference by powerful outsiders, for example influential organizations external to the LAS such as the Department of Health and the Regional Health Authority, plus government-led changes in the NHS and resistance from trade unions.

Developments within the government sector can provide many examples of externally set deadlines that bear little relation to the practical realities of systems development. The Field System and the Poll Tax developments in the UK both illustrate this problem, while in the USA a study by the GAO (1988) found that 'unrealistic time schedules set by others' was a major factor in a large number of government projects. This problem is not, however, confined to government projects since aggressive 'deadline management' by senior managers is common practice within all parts of the industry.

Internal Power Struggles

Perhaps the worst thing that can happen, in a political sense, to a development is for it to become the symbol of a wider power struggle between competing groups within an organization. Once this occurs it will become increasingly difficult to get an accurate 'reality check' on the true state of the project. Information systems may move from being regarded as solutions to business problems to being seen as symbols of power and influence that must be either reinforced or undermined according to your point of view.

External Power Struggles

Many organizations find themselves in wider power struggles as they seek to establish an advantage over their competitors and establish themselves in their chosen market. In this struggle appearances are vitally important, and organizations will go to great lengths to ensure that they are not seen as 'losers' by either their competitors or their market. In this context IS developments may not be allowed to fail and organizations may persist with troubled projects simply because the political and commercial implications are too awful to contemplate.

Critical Failure Factors—Conduct of the Project

Initiation Phase

Technology-focused developments

The London Ambulance Service case is a perfect example of technology-focused development in which far more energy appeared to have been expended upon the technical rather than the human factors of the system. While the stereotypical image of the 'techie' who is happier dealing with technology than people has probably never been true, it does illustrate a problem that manifests itself as a lack of organizational focus. It was not that the LAS development did not consider the human resource issues of the development, but rather that they were seen as peripheral to the main technology-related business in hand. Despite the difficulties with the development, once the focus of the new system was fixed on the technology, staff objections were always likely to be viewed as trouble-making rather than throw doubt upon the system itself. The original design for the Taurus system illustrated a similar naivety since the technical solution first presented totally ignored the financial and political realities of the market it was intended to serve.

The danger of technology-focused developments is that within their rational world they are perfectly consistent and feasible. The problem is that success in the technical sphere alone is not enough. For a system to

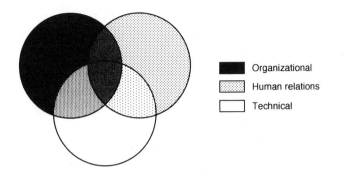

Figure 7.4 Triple focus required for an information system to be successful

be truly successful it must maintain a triple focus on the organizational, human relations and technical spheres in which it operates, as illustrated in Figure 7.4.

The lure of the leading edge

It is the received wisdom in the IT industry that technology can give organizations a competitive edge in the marketplace. And so it can, in some circumstances. What is by no means certain however, is that the latest technology will always provide an edge to any organization that implements it. Yet it is implicit in much of the way in which technology is discussed that the newer the technology or technique, the bigger will be the competitive edge to be obtained. This is not the case and it must surely be a question of the appropriate use of technology.

It is in the nature of IT that it is continually improving. But there is a big difference between staying within the known envelope of technology and working on the leading edge. The big difference is risk— not for nothing is working with the very latest software or hardware in novel applications also known as being at the 'bleeding edge'. The question that must be asked of all proposals to work at the leading edge must be 'is it really necessary?'. Given the inherently higher levels of uncertainty attached to leading-edge developments, organizations must ask themselves whether their goals could be achieved using mainstream technology.

In fact the first question that should be asked of the performance of any proposed system is simply 'Is it proven or is it promises?' While within virtually every development there will always be an element of 'promises' rather than proof, it is vital to get the balance in favour of proven performance. The experiences of the London Ambulance Service and the Performing Right Society both illustrate the dangers of working on promises rather than a proven track record with developments that were central to their activities. Such an approach was always going to be a high-risk strategy. Risk will always be a part of new information systems developments, but the level of acceptable risk will vary according to the application. The use of the latest technology to create and exploit new markets will always be a recognizably risky venture, whereas it is probably safer for the creation of systems to despatch ambulances and administer royalty payments to be risk averse.

> When it comes to buying technology, it often pays to be second. That way you are more likely to end up with a 747 than a Spruce Goose (*The Economist*, 1993).

Complexity underestimated

A feature that emerges in many of the cases examined is the apparent failure, in the early planning stages, to appreciate fully the complexity of the development as a whole. Although such a lack of detailed understanding of the intricate nature of the project is likely to lead to problems later, it may be a predictable outcome from the project-initiation process.

In order for any proposal to turn into a funded project development it will almost certainly have to pass through the feasibility stage and gain budget approval. However, in order to ensure that the project gains approval, there will be a tendency for its supporters to understate its complexity—with obvious repercussions on the budget, date of implementation and even its eventual success or failure. At some stage however, this lack of initial understanding will be revealed by the unforeseen problems and timescale slippages that will occur. These are warning signs that should not be ignored. However, while such an understating of complexity may be reasonably expected in a leading-edge application and should thus be anticipated, it can only be a danger sign for a mainstream development.

Analysis and Design Phase

Poor consultation

Inadequate consultation with the major stakeholders of a proposed system during the analysis phase is a high-risk strategy. That it is sometimes unavoidable—as in the case of The Field System, when the client group had yet to be formed—does not make it any the less risky. In such cases it is probably better to defer the system rather than run the risk of creating a system that will not be used. At the same time a consultation process that has form but lacks any real substance is just as dangerous.

The LAS case illustrated how a key group—the ambulance staff—were marginalized throughout the analysis and design phase with the effect that they made little contribution to the shape of the final system. This lack of any real involvement at any early stage led to persistent objections to the operation of the system itself as it began to be tested, which were in turn ignored and undermined.

Design by committee[9]

Committee work is probably among the most political of business activities, as anyone with experience of such work knows only too well the power struggles, making and breaking of alliances and game playing that can take place. For committees within individual organizations the primary goal—say, long-term success for the company—is likely to be shared, although there is likely to be some disagreement about the way in which this should be achieved—the means. When committees are formed from groups drawn from different organizations there is likely to be disagreement about both the goals and the means, with the result that the intensity of the power struggles, alliances and game playing that takes place is an order of magnitude greater. Creating a viable system under such circumstances is likely to be very difficult indeed, as illustrated by the Confirm and Taurus cases.

These cases demonstrate the dangers of attempting to design a system when the goals of those involved are not only very different but may actually conflict. If those involved are also not fully committed to the

———· · · · · · · ·

[9] While the points made in this section relate to committees made up of potential business competitors they are probably just as applicable to inter-departmental or inter-divisional design committees.

success of the system there may be little or no need to compromise on their particular aims in order to ensure the success of the system as a whole. Indeed, the final design for the Taurus system shows strong evidence of this behaviour. A further complication is that a system may reach a stage when many of those on the committee, perhaps having lost earlier battles, may prefer to see the entire development fail rather than concede on their own objectives. A side effect of the committee approach is that it may become difficult to draw a line under the design process, with changes to the system being demanded even when the development is quite advanced.

Technical 'fix' for a management problem

Technology will not, on its own, provide a solution for a management problem. Organizational change cannot be successfully achieved simply by using technology to 'fix' a knotty problem, as was attempted at the LAS when the new despatch system was used to enforce changes to staff working practices. The VBA case is another example in which technology was to be used to fix a problem that was in fact caused by chronic understaffing. The selection of the technological 'fix' for intractable management problems is always likely to be a high-risk strategy.

Poor procurement

The LAS case is also a good example of how a procurement procedure could be followed to the letter and yet still result in a poor decision. While this in some ways a rather obvious point, it should not be too surprising how staff with specialist procurement experience, albeit in an unrelated area, should be involved in the decision to acquire high-technology systems.

Development Phase

Staff turnover

Staff turnover is to be expected within all projects and, provided it is relatively low, should be manageable and not unduly affect the progress or subsequent completion of a development. However, regular and recurrent staff turnover is a triple signal. First, there may be something going badly wrong with the project, and that staff may be baling out while they still can. Second, staff morale may be collapsing due to management or project problems. Third, project deadlines are unlikely to be met due to the delays in getting replacement staff in post and up to speed on the project. It is not for nothing that Fred Brooks referred to personnel turnover in complex systems developments as a 'disaster'.

Competency

The issue of technical competency is really quite hard for non-technical managers to assess, other than by looking at the quality of the results—by which time it may be too late. Problems surrounding the design, development, project management and quality assurance in all the cases discussed here are apparent. It is not enough to say that only these areas deserve special attention, rather it indicates that extreme care is taken in the appointment of staff and that the use of low-key project reviews (as a form of QA procedure) at important stages in the development should always be an option.

Split sites

The game of Chinese whispers, in which a phrase passed from person to person changes its meaning completely, illustrates the kind of problems caused by working over split sites. Certainly some of the split-site problems faced by both the Taurus and Confirm projects may have been significant factors in the failure of the developments. Working over split sites is not, in itself, a guarantee of problems, rather it increases the chances that two types of difficulties will arise: communication problems and work group problems.

Communication problems between split sites are probably inevitable but can be minimized through regular contact through meetings, e-mail or video conferences. Workgroup problems due to rivalry and political infighting can also be helped by improved communications, with short-term staff exchanges being of positive benefit to eliminate the kind of difficulties that can arise.

Implementation Phase

Receding deadlines

Once a project begins to miss milestones or deadlines repeatedly, alarm bells should start to ring in the heads of those responsible for the development. This one factor is perhaps the most powerful single indicator that a project may be in trouble and that it may be time to take a closer look. Of this problem Fred Brooks (1982) has written:

> When one hears of disastrous schedule slippage in a project, he imagines that a series of major calamities must have befallen it. Usually, however, the disaster is due to termites, not tornadoes; and the schedule has slipped imperceptibly but inexorably. Indeed, major calamities are easier to handle; one responds with major force, radical reorganization, the invention of new approaches. The whole team rises to the occasion.
> But the day-by-day slippage is harder to recognize, harder to prevent, harder to make up.

Just about every case of project failure that has been examined repeatedly missed deadlines. Some missed so many deadlines and went on for so long that they turned failures into disasters. It must be stressed, however, that a missed deadline is not in itself a sure-fire indicator that a project is going to fail. However, the more often it happens, the greater the doubt it throws onto the eventual success of the project since it may be the symptom of a more serious condition.

Testing and training—the poor relations of systems development?

Inadequate testing and poor training are the classic signs of development that is under pressure and not fully in control. Often regarded as unsexy afterthoughts to the mainstream development process, they may be viewed as second-class jobs that 'fit in' with the rest of the process. In fact, this is far from what their real status within a project should be.

A well-designed and correctly implemented testing regime is perhaps the best ally management can have in ensuring that a system performs as expected. The Confirm and Taurus cases both illustrate how failed systems tests can become the catalyst that initiates a chain of events culminating in the premature closure of a project. At the other extreme, the LAS case shows just what can happen when a testing and training programme suffers in the rush to meet a tight deadline.

The events at the LAS are the nightmare scenario of thousands of development teams who, faced with inadequate time to test fully due to project slippage, have gone live with a partially tested system—the errors that are subsequently discovered then being dealt with during 'systems maintenance'. While such an approach means that a system has apparently been completed on 'time' and possibly to 'budget', the reality is that the users end up testing the system and the errors that are uncovered still have to be fixed. This does nothing to inspire user confidence in the new system and undermines the credibility of the development team.

A good training programme is hard to get right and very easy to get wrong. Once project deadlines begin to slip, pre-implementation activities, such as training, need to be moved to accommodate the changes. If this not done staff will be trained well before the system is due to go live, with the result that the impact of the training will be reduced and much of what has been learnt will have been forgotten. The LAS case is a perfect, if depressing, example of what can happen if staff are not given 'refresher' training before a system finally goes live.

FINAL VARIATION

Picking over wreckage of failed information systems developments contained within this book it is notable that, although we have been presented with the known facts of each of the cases examined, we have rarely heard from any of the non-IS managers involved. The following case rectifies that situation and concludes with a piece of advice we could all do well to heed.

Pineapple Group plc[10]

Former leading model Debbie Moore started a business running dance studios in 1979 and took Pineapple Group public in 1982. In March 1988 she bought out the original dance and fashion part of the business. The remaining public company was bought by Doctus, a marketing and management consultancy, for £44 million in 1989. Pineapple Limited, the private company, has a turnover of £3 million. In this case Debbie

[10] This was originally published as part of the 'My Biggest Mistake' series in *The Independent on Sunday*, 4 March 1990.

Moore relates her experiences with the acquisition of a computerized inventory management system.

> In business you make many mistakes and in retrospect one of my biggest—which was a recurring one—was not to stick to my convictions when I knew instinctively something was wrong. As I say in my book *When a Woman Means Business*, one of the golden rules is 'don't rely on the experts'.
>
> When I was Chairman of Pineapple Group plc, alongside the dance studios and fitness business, we were a rapidly expanding fashion business and needed to computerize our systems. I am not very computer literate and had only ever used the basics.
>
> We were approached by a company which came recommended. They told us they were offering us a package which they had installed for Speedo, a clothing and swimwear company. The main things that the system was supposed to do were to keep control of the stock, to monitor sales by style and colour and do invoicing. They said Speedo were satisfied with the system and, although their business was slightly simpler than ours, we decided to go ahead.
>
> I wanted to keep the manual systems as backup. The accountancy advisers just let them go because they thought the new computerized systems would be implemented fairly quickly. They told me that this was therefore unnecessary. I was lulled into a false sense of security and didn't insist.
>
> The consultant, a 'computer genius', was set up in an open-plan office at our warehouse on the Holloway Road, north London. I knew something was wrong because the consultant, who was costing us a vast amount of money, was always on the phone to the software company, and there was no information coming through. We didn't have stock analysis or sales figures and time was going by—and we had lost our manual system. Also, people started calling up saying that they had received the wrong order or that the invoices were incorrect, which, of course, meant delays in payments. The consultant was clearly having problems—he seemed to be smoking more and more. (Wherever he was standing he was surrounded by at least 30 cigarette ends.)
>
> At this point I insisted that the computer must be faulty. The

computer expert and all the accountants and the financial people—
which you get when you're a plc and shed when you go private—
thought this was a hilarious statement. They were astonished that,
after three months of work, I even dared to say it. 'What did I
know about computers?' they asked. Consequently, at the time I
thought it wasn't the right thing to have said and I left the expert
to get on with it again.

We had the computer for the best part of nine months and it
never worked properly. We only found out there really was a
problem when the consultant left the company. Then he came to
us to say that he could help with all the things that had gone
wrong. This was the first time that anyone admitted that the
package we had was not the same as the one which had been in use
at Speedo, but a modified version (which had never worked before
or since).

In the end the whole operation cost about £100 000 for the
hardware, software and the cost of the consultant (not to mention
the time involved) which contributed to our losses that year.

It was a fairly crucial mistake, but a difficult one to avoid as we
had done everything by the book and seen the system in operation.
How were we to know that they would put in a different system?
As soon as I was suspicious I should have implemented the manual
system again and insisted that someone else come in to have a look
at the computer.

Common sense should prevail in a business and you must always
be insistent and not be undermined by the 'experts'.

(Reproduced by permission of *The Independent on Sunday*.)

Afterword: The Way Forward

The cases in this book probably represents the tip of a very large iceberg
of IS failure. For one reason or another, each of the cases we have
examined hit the headlines and some of the circumstances surrounding
each failure became known. This is the exception to the rule. Talk to
anyone who has been involved for even a few years with the use of IT
in organizations and you will realize that a lot more IS failures are

quietly buried than ever see the light of day. As has been discussed earlier in this book and elsewhere, this situation must not be allowed to continue indefinitely—the industry needs to grow up and start learning from its mistakes instead of pretending they never happened.

The CFFs outlined above are intended to be a first step rather than the definitive set of failure factors. Development of a shared understanding of past mistakes, and the means by which they may be avoided, can be achieved only if wider and more detailed scrutiny and analysis of failures is possible.

References

Block, R., *The Politics of Projects*, Yourdon Press, New York (1983).

Brooks, F., *The Mythical Man-Month: Essays on Software Engineering*, Addison-Wesley, Reading, MA (1982).

Brooks, F., 'No silver bullet: essence and accidents of software engineering', *Computer*, April (1987).

Corbato, F., 'On building systems that will fail', *Communications of the ACM* 34, No. 9, September, 79 (1992).

Drummond, H., 'Escalation in organizational decision-making: a case of recruiting an incompetent employee', *Journal of Behavioural Decision Making*, 7, 43–55 (1994).

Drummond, H., 'De-escalation in decision-making: a case of a disastrous partnership', *Journal of Management Studies* 32(3), May, 265–81 (1995).

The Economist, 'All fall down', 20 March (1993).

GAO, *An Evaluation of the Grand Design Approach to Developing Computer-based Application Systems*, September (1988).

Handy, C., *Understanding Organizations*, 4th edn, Penguin, Harmondsworth (1993).

Rochlin, G. I., 'Iran Air Flight 655 and the USS Vincennes: complex, large-scale military systems and the failure of control' in La Porte, T. R. (ed.) *Social Responses to Large Technical Systems: Control or Anticipation* (Kluwer, Dordrecht, 1991).

Staw, B. and Ross, J., 'Knowing when to pull the plug', *Harvard Business Review*, March–April (1987a).

Staw, B. and Ross, J., 'Behaviour in escalation situations: antecedents, prototypes and solutions', in Cummings, L. and Staw, B. (eds), *Research in Organization Behaviour*, JAI Press, Greenwich, CT (1987b).

ANNOTATED
BIBLIOGRAPHY
. . . .

T his selective bibliography is designed to provide a starting point for those who wish to find out more about the whole area of information systems failure and makes no claims to being a comprehensive view of the entire literature in the area. The review has been structured according to the five major themes of causes and cases of IS failure, progress through failure, project management and the inherent risks of computer technology. While this structure is to some extent arbitrary, it is intended to provide readers new to the area with a means of focusing their research efforts. In order to create a perspective for the above material, the bibliography starts with a section on software engineering practice.

1 Software Engineering Practice

Software engineering is a complex and technical domain with books in the area being aimed at the software professional and, for this reason, tend to be pretty hard going for the non-technical manager. This caveat aside, the books listed below contain a wealth of useful information on the theory and practice of software engineering.

Software Engineering: A Practitioner's Approach, Roger Pressman, McGraw-Hill (1992). A comprehensive and highly rated text widely recommended within universities.
Strategies for Software Engineering: The Management of Risk and Quality, Martyn A. Ould, John Wiley (1990). A readable book intended for software professionals that draws on the author's own extensive experience.

Other texts with a comprehensive coverage that are recommended include:

Software Engineering: Principles and Practice, Hans van Vliet, John Wiley (1993)
Software Engineering, Ian Sommerville, Addison-Wesley (1996).

A text that takes a rather less specialist view on the whole software engineering process and presents a readable account of the many issues involved in the creation of an information system from a mainstream management perspective is:

Computerising Work, Leslie Willcocks and David Mason, Paradigm Publishing (1987).

2   IS Failures—Causes

The books listed below include some of the classic works in the area, with the publications by Lucas and Brooks being of particular note.

Why Information Systems Fail, Henry C. Lucas, Jr, Columbia University Press (1975). An early academic study of IS failures that, while not the most readable of books, is a classic in this area.

The Universal Elixir and other Computing Projects Which Failed, Robert L. Glass, *Computerworld* (1977). A series of anonymized cases that serve to demonstrate many of the reasons IS developments fail. Slightly dated, but still worth reading.

The Mythical Man-Month, Frederick P. Brooks, Jr, Addison-Wesley (1975). An oft-cited text that provides a highly readable account of the many problems that may be encountered in developing an information system. One of the few classic texts in this area. A 20th anniversary edition was published in 1995 that included two new chapters, including the essay 'No silver bullet: essence and accidents of software engineering'. Highly recommended.

Why Information Systems Fail: A Case Study Approach, Chris Sauer, Alfred Waller (1993). A detailed academic examination of IS failure that combines some detailed case histories in addition to providing a useful overview of academic literature in the area.

3   IS Failures—Cases

For those who wish to read about rather more recent IS failures the sources of information open to us are usually more limited and more unreliable than we would wish. However, one shaft of light into the usually closed world of IS failure is the Government Inquiry. The reports published by the GAO in the USA and the NAO in the UK provide a detailed insight into the management of government IS projects that usually has no commercial parallel, and for this reason they make fascinating reading. The verbatim proceedings of the Public

Accounts Committee in the UK, a body of MPs empowered to question government officials involved in failed IS projects on their actions, provides a still more interesting insight into the organizational context and managerial responsibilities surrounding such IS developments. It is a shame that the failed IS developments of commercial organizations are not subject to the same open examination.

The reports of the GAO in the USA generally take a much wider, more strategic view than those of the UK NAO. However, both provide detailed (if sometimes rather dry) accounts of proposed or current IS developments and are a major source of reliable data in an area in which hard facts are notoriously hard to come by.

United States General Accounting Office, Washington, DC, 20548, USA
National Audit Office, HMSO, London
House of Commons, Committee of Public Accounts, HMSO, London

The major source of information about IS failures comes from the specialist trade and mainstream newspapers. However, it must be recognized that the constraints of space and the need to excite the interest of the readership do not allow for detailed coverage or analysis. Nonetheless, this information, if it is treated with appropriate caution, does provide a rich seam of useful anecdotal evidence that practitioners can learn from. Publications that will typically carry such case information include:

Information Week
Computerworld
Computer Weekly
Computing

4 Learning from Failure

The following books all demonstrate how progress, at least partly, depends on a thorough understanding of how failures occur.

To *Engineer is Human: The Role of Failure in Successful Design*, Henry Petroski, Macmillan (1985). This book should be required reading for everyone involved in IS development activity. A highly readable text. A classic.

Catastrophic Failures, Victor Bignell, Geoff Peters and Christopher Pym, Open University Press (1977).

Understanding Systems Failures, Victor Bignell and Joyce Fortune, Manchester University Press (1984). These two books provide a series of detailed analyses of major disasters and give a vivid demonstration of how a series of small errors can, given the right circumstances, develop into a major failure. Fascinating reading.

Learning from Failure: The systems approach, Joyce Fortune and Geoff Peters, John Wiley (1995). Based on the authors research into how failures in organizations can be understood, this readable rather academic book also introduces the Systems Failures Method of failure avoidance.

5   Managing IS Projects

The literature surrounding the subject of project management is very large and the list below is intended to represent a starting point for those interested in the area.

The Politics of Projects, Robert Block, Yourdon Press (1983). For those who are interested in the political context of the information systems development process, this is the book to read.

Winning at Project Management: What works, What Fails and Why, Robert D. Gilbreath, John Wiley (1986). This book documents the many problems inherent in managing projects and presents a huge array of potential project problems and pitfalls. Very readable, it should be of great benefit to any practitioner in the field.

The Anatomy of Major Projects, Peter Morris and George Hough, John Wiley (1987). Case-based discussion of a series of large-scale projects that provides a detailed analysis of their success and failure.

6   Risks Inherent in Computer Technology

Those of us who work with computers will recognize that many of the problems that we face on a day-to-day basis are due to the special nature of the technology. The following sources provide a useful exploration of the nature of these problems and highlight the special challenges they pose.

Digital Woes, Lauren Wiener, Addison-Wesley (1993). A highly readable book that highlights the problems posed by the increasing complexity of the software that is at the heart of all information systems.

Computer Related Risks, Peter G. Neumann, Addison-Wesley (1995). Compiled from the RISKS forum, this book provides a systematic and informed analysis of the many and varied problems computer technology has brought in its wake. Anyone who has a blind faith in the power of computer technology should read this book.

Computer Ethics: Cautionary Tales and Ethical Dilemmas in Computing, T. Forester & P. Morrison, Blackwell (1990). Making many of the same points about software as *Digital Woes*, this book also includes an interesting and informed discussion about the ethics surrounding the development of information systems.

Normal Accidents: Living with High-Risk Technologies, C. Perrow, Basic Books (1984). This book is a reasoned and well-supported development of the premise that unforeseen (and possibly unforeseeable) accidents are an inevitable result of the increasing complexity of modern technological systems. Based around a series of case histories, this is a classic book in the genre.

Comp.risks. This is a moderated forum dedicated to exploring the risks of computer technology. Compulsive reading, it is available over Usenet or by subscription. The entire RISKS archive is also available on-line by anonymous ftp.

GLOSSARY

ACAS   Arbitration, Conciliation and Advisory Service.

AVLS   Automated Vehicle Location System, sub-system used within the London Ambulance Service Computer-Aided Despatch system.

ATM   Automatic Teller Machine.

Bespoke software   Software written, generally as a one-off, for a specific application.

Big Bang   Term usually used to refer to the first phase of automation of the share trading process within the London Stock Exchange. It was derived from its other meaning, that of the 'overnight change' method of moving from an old to a new computerized information system.

CAD   Term used to refer to the Computer Aided Despatch system developed by the London Ambulance Service. May also be used to refer to Computer Aided Design.

CAC   Central Ambulance Control.

CEO   Chief Executive Officer. In the UK the same post is generally referred to as Managing Director.

CIO   Chief Information Officer. In the UK the same post is generally referred to as IT Director.

CRS   Computer Reservation System.

CASE   Computer Aided Software Engineering.

CASE tool   System designed to automate one or more stages of the software development process.

Critical Failure Factor   A factor that may be associated with, and thus may be used to predict, the failure of an IS development.

Downsizing   A term originally used to refer to the process of moving applications to smaller computer systems, i.e. mainframe to minicomputer or a minicomputer to a microcomputer. May also be used as a generic term to refer to a reduction in size, i.e. downsizing of a workforce.

Dematerialization   A term used in the second (Taurus) phase of the automation of the share trading at the London Stock Exchange to refer to the move from paper share certificates to computerized records of shareholdings.

DES   Data Encryption Standard, and IBM developed data encryption system.

GAO   General Accounting Office.

GSA   General Services Administration.

IRS   Internal Revenue Service.

Implementation   The stage in the lifecycle of an IS development in which a new system enters into the operational environment and goes 'live'.

LAS   London Ambulance Service.

Mainframe computer   Very powerful computer system capable of supporting a very large number of users and applications simultaneously. As technology improves, the distinction between mainframe and mini-computers has become increasingly blurred.

Methodology   A combination of tools, techniques and rules designed to improve the IS development process.

Minicomputer   Powerful computer system capable of supporting a large number of users and applications simultaneously.

MDT   Mobile Data Terminals. Sub-system used within the London Ambulance Service Computer-Aided Despatch system.

NAO National Audit Office.

NHS National Health Service.

NUPE National Union of Public Employees. No longer in existence, now subsumed within the trade union UNISON.

OLTP On-Line Transaction Processing.

Outsourcing The contracting of an internal operation or system, such as payroll, order processing or maintenance, to an outside supplier.

Packaged software Standard software, usually generic in nature, created by a specialist organization that is generally licensed from its originator. Sometimes also referred to as 'shrink-wrapped' software.

PIR Project Issue Report. Part of a software quality assurance system that is designed to identify and track the resolution of software errors.

POISE procurement of information systems effectively. Procurement methodology used in the NHS.

PRINCE Projects In Controlled Environments, project management methodology.

PRS Performing Right Society. An organization that, in the UK, collects performance royalties for music copyright holders.

QA Quality Assurance. A term used to refer to the systems and processes of ensuring that software, or any other item, is of the correct quality.

RHA Regional Health Authority.

RIFS Radio Interface System. Sub-system used within the London Ambulance Service Computer Aided Despatch system.

RISP Regional Information Systems Plan. Title given to the information systems development undertaken by the Wessex Regional Health Authority.

SE   Stock Exchange (London).

SSADM   Structured Systems Analysis and Design Methodology.

SRS   Systems Requirement Specification. A set of requirements, usually in the form a document, that express the performance and operational requirements of an information system. The SRS is usually the end product of the systems analysis stage.

Siscot   Securities and Investments Steering Committee on Taurus. Committee, composed of representatives of the banking, stockbroking and share registrar communities, that was set up to agree the requirements for the Taurus system.

Sepon   Stock Exchange Pool Nominee, an organization that, under the Taurus system, would have held records of share ownership on behalf of clients and others.

Systems analysis   That part of the systems development process concerned with investigating and recording the needs of users and other stakeholders in order that they may be reflected in the design of a new system.

TEC   Training and Education Council. UK government agency responsible for the provision of training and education.

TFS   The Field System.

UNIX   Multi-user, multi-tasking computer operating system widely used in minicomputer environments.

VBA   Veterans Benefit Administration.

INDEX